THE MASTER PLAN OF TEACHING

THE
MASTER
PLAN OF
TEACHING

MATT FRIEDEMAN

VICTOR BOOKS®

A DIVISION OF SCRIPTURE PRESS PUBLICATIONS INC.
USA CANADA ENGLAND

Unless otherwise noted, Scripture quotations are from *New American Standard Bible,* © the Lockman Foundation 1960, 1962, 1963, 1968, 1971, 1972, 1973, 1975, 1977. Other quotations are taken from the *Revised Standard Version of the Bible* (RSV), © 1946, 1952, 1971, 1973; those marked NIV are from the *Holy Bible, New International Version,* © 1973, 1978, 1984, International Bible Society. Used by permission of Zondervan Bible Publishers; verses marked TLB are taken from *The Living Bible,* © 1971, Tyndale House Publishers, Wheaton, IL 60189. Used by permission.

Library of Congress Cataloging-in-Publication Data
Friedeman, Matt.
    The master plan of teaching / by Matt Friedeman.
        p.   cm.
    Includes bibliographical references.
    ISBN 0-89693-767-4
    1. Jesus Christ—Teaching. 2. Christian education—   Philosophy. 3. Christian education—Teaching methods. I. Title.
    BT590.T5F75   1990
    268—dc20   89-48779
                                                                                            CIP

CONTENTS

ACKNOWLEDGMENTS

A number of people participated in the process resulting in this book and gave valuable suggestions. Dr. John Guenther of the University of Kansas allowed me the privilege of completing a dissertation topic on similar material, which aided in gathering data for this manuscript. Dr. Allan Coppedge participated in that process as well and taught me many of the valuable concepts contained within these pages. Dr. Bill Arnold and Dr. Ray Easley of Wesley Biblical Seminary read the manuscript and offered their suggestions—some of which I took and others I probably should have! Lisa Ausley offered several comments that were extremely valuable. Martha Boardman served as a proof-reader, just one more effort of love from my mother-in-law. Keith Tonkel helped with this project too, and his life, along with that of Wells Church, continues to enrich my life in ways immeasurable. And, of course, Robert Hosack of Victor Books—a terrific editor.

I do not simply acknowledge my wife and son Caleb. I bow down to God in praise!

To all these and others too numerous to mention—thanks!
Matt Friedeman

To my teachers.
Those who really took the time:

My bride Mary
My folks—Jerry and Janis Friedeman
My brothers and sister—Dick, Lisa, Todd, and Kent
My Aunt Aleta
Loren and Marilyn Dyke
Coach Don Duncan
Coach Bob Timmons
Coach Keith Kephart
Paul Law
Professor Al Coppedge
Reverend Keith Tonkel
And close friends, too numerous to list

FOREWORD

Jesus calls us to be His disciples. "Take My yoke upon you," He says, "and learn of Me" (Matt. 11:29). The invitation is to follow Him, who, to use the translating of Grotins, is "the Example, the Teacher, the Giver of eternal life" (John 14:6).

While this discipleship has a beginning, it never ends. Every day confronts us with new discovery and challenge. And as we apply to our heart what we learn, we have the joy of being progressively conformed to His likeness, "from glory to glory, even as by the Spirit of the Lord" (2 Cor. 3:18).

By placing the emphasis on becoming like Him, the Master assures us that we not only grow in His character, but also participate in His ministry. No one can follow Jesus without someway becoming involved in what He does.

Disciples, then, if they are properly taught, inevitably mature into disciplers. In turn, as the new believers do the same, through the process of multiplication, God's good news of salvation will ultimately reach every tongue and tribe and nation.

The Great Commission brings this strategy into focus. It is not a special call nor a gift of the Spirit; it is a way of life—the way that our Lord chose to direct His steps while He lived among us, and now the way that He asks His disciples to follow.

What makes the plan so potentially powerful through the Spirit is that every Christian can have a part. The priesthood of all believers takes relevant form in daily conduct.

Yet, tragically, in our preoccupation with formal programs of education, we have largely missed the dynamics of Jesus' discipleship. Not that we deny His approach, but that we are too wrapped up in other things to pay the price.

Following the way of Jesus in making disciples is costly. To take it seriously means to renounce our own rights in loving submission to His. There is a cross in it—a commitment to do the will of God, whatever it takes.

That finally is the bottom line of this book. There is much pertinent information here in educational principles, to be sure; and how these concepts relate to practical training is given particular attention; but through it all can be heard a summons to put our lives on the line.

Matt Friedeman has earned the right to be heard. He is schooled in the professional art of teaching, having studied the theories and researched the methods of the trade. But preeminently he is a disciple of the Master, still learning to measure his values by the priorities of the Kingdom.

I can learn much from such a man. Believing, too, that any student of Christ can have the same experience, it is a pleasure to commend the book to you.

Robert E. Coleman
Trinity Evangelical Divinity School
Deerfield, Illinois

*He was often a healer, sometimes a worker
of signs, frequently a preacher,
but always a teacher. . . .
Teaching was his chief business.*
                                    —John A. Marquis

*Let us run with endurance the race that is set
·before us, fixing our eyes on Jesus.*
                                    —The Epistle to the Hebrews

As Christian educators we would be wise to fix our eyes upon Jesus—teacher par excellence. In Him we can find our objectives, the foundation for our methodology, the working stuff of our craft. The ethical question, "What would Jesus do?" becomes the educational inquiry, "How would Jesus teach?"

CHAPTER ONE

FIXING OUR EYES ON JESUS: TEACHER PAR EXCELLENCE

E Stanley Jones was weary. The famed missionary to India had labored hard for the Lord in his adopted homeland, yet he found his physical, emotional, and spiritual resources depleted. After eight and one half years on the field he was ordered back to America to rest and regain perspective. Following what seemed a very brief furlough, spent lecturing and studying, Jones was sent back to India. He later admitted that his reticent reaction was simply, "I'm not ready."

But he did return. Almost immediately upon his arrival, however, the vast responsibilities overwhelmed him and sent him again into retreat, this time to the mountains for a time of recuperation. Jones frankly admitted that his inner experience was not sustaining the outer trappings of spirituality. He conceded that "the game was up—I would have to leave the mission field and my work and try to regain my shattered health." In that darkest of hours, God spoke to this missionary and asked if he were indeed ready for the work to which he was called. "No, Lord—I'm done for," came the reply. "I've reached the end of my resources and I can't go on." As Jones recounts in his spiritual autobiography, *A Song of Ascents,* God then promised, "If you'll turn the problem over to Me and not worry about it, I'll take care of it." The eager reply? "Lord, I close the deal right here."[1] He took God at His word.

Jones was transformed. He went from tired to tireless. His ministry from that point on seemed supernaturally empowered, and reverberations from his Spirit-inspired preaching and writing are being heard even today. In retrospect, Jones admitted that the remarkable turnabout in his life came when he realized the simplicity of his calling. At the outset of his career, the young missionary had tried to "bob up and down the line" defending his neatly packaged theological positions. He fielded questions and objections about Moses and David, Jesus and Paul, Western civilization and the Christian Church. It was too much for any one man, despite oratorical gifts and intellectual capacity. The result? A worn and weary warrior was forced to retreat. Jones writes:

I was worried. There was no well defined issue. I found the battle almost invariably being pitched at one of these three places: the Old Testament, or Western Civilization, or the Christian Church. I had the ill-defined but instinctive feeling that the heart of the matter was being left out. Then I saw that I could, and should, shorten my line, that I could take my stand at Christ and before that non-Christian world refuse to know anything save Jesus Christ and Him crucified. . . . Then I saw that there is where I should have been all the time. I saw that the Gospel lies in the person of Jesus . . . my task was simplified.[2]

Jones found it not only simplified, but vitalized. It wasn't that the Old Testament didn't matter any more, or that doctrinal understanding was of no account. Quite the contrary, it meant that theology and his understanding of revelation be held up to the light of Christ and placed under the constant corrective of His person. Jones was convinced that only from that perspective could doctrine, thought, and action be kept pure and effective for today's world.

Implications for the Teacher

The same approach commends itself to today's Christian teacher. We can easily be overwhelmed with the heavy responsibility of our task, or muddled by the multitude of methods touted by education experts. And we may become paranoid because curriculum advertising has effectively made us feel "out of it" if we don't have the latest materials. Feelings of inadequacy may dissuade many of us from even attempting to undertake the vital task of teaching God's people. As Christian educators we would be wise, therefore, to "fix our eyes upon Jesus" — Teacher par excellence. In Him we can find our objectives, the foundation for our methodology, the working stuff of our craft. The ethical question, "What would Jesus do?" becomes the educational inquiry, "How would Jesus teach?" If we dare to ask so bold a question and adjust our character, objectives, and methodologies to match, then like E. Stanley Jones we will arise from the place of prayer with our task simplified and revitalized.

I can speak from experience for I have felt such a surge of refreshment. I devoted several years of my life to graduate work studying the educational arts. There students and professors alike engaged in intense examination of educational technique, philosophy, research methodology, and history. But as with all graduate students, there were times when I looked up bleary eyed from well-marked texts and heavily scrawled notepads to wonder how all this inquiry fit together. After several years of school and oodles of facts, figures, and philosophies rebounding off my cranium, I found myself much like the missionary Jones. I was tired.

The mental exhaustion came to a head when I was awarded a position on a graduate research team. For this project, a colleague and I were asked to roam the vast recesses of our library in search of specific behaviors that made for an "effective instructor." Off to the book stacks we strode, expecting to compile a significant twenty-item list by day's end. No such luck. Some two weeks later we emerged with an enormous inventory of 435 different statements suggesting ways to improve classroom instruction. They covered everything from how to write on the chalkboard to appropriate dress in the schoolhouse. Adding to the perplexity of the task were the contradictions we encountered midst the research. Though each claimed to be backed by empirical evidence, many of the 435 behaviors refuted each other.

I remember sitting at home one evening at my word processor, entering some of our numerous findings. I had reached a point where it was more than necessary to take a break. Sitting in my lounge chair with Coke in hand, I reflected upon how complicated this science (it no longer felt like an art) of education had become over my years of graduate work. I had taken countless courses, compiled mountains of research, and had performed well under the tutelage of my advisor. But my mind was boggled and I knew that I was in danger of fulfilling the destiny of all too many Ph.D.s: to know more and more about less and less until I knew everything about nothing. It was tiring; it was frustrating; it was time to talk to God.

There may well be 435 appropriate behaviors for effective teaching. In fact, if we get really picky, that figure probably doesn't even scratch the surface. But what I needed that night in my living room, and what I continue to desire, is a focus, a center—a place where I can find my identity as the teacher I was meant to be. I prayed a short but intense prayer and asked the Lord to help me reaffirm Him as my Ideal.

Since that night I have tried to concentrate on Jesus the Teacher as my model. That is not to denigrate current educational research. Much of it is valid and can help us hone our skills as effective communicators. But there are still times when I sit at my computer keyboard, several books and journals ajar, frantically trying to compose a lecture before the deadline. When I feel myself sliding toward that mind-boggled state reminiscent of my graduate school days, I can always trust the Holy Spirit to prick my memory and get the Center in focus.

I sincerely doubt I will ever have the world-wide impact of an E. Stanley Jones. But I can relate in a small way to his Answer to the overwhelming dilemma that nearly cut short a brilliant ministry. I know what the person of Jesus, and a desire to imitate Him, has done for my perspective on education. Research findings come and go, to be refuted or refined at later dates. Jesus the Teacher, however, provides us an example of excellence for eternity.

Jesus the Teacher

In seeking to emulate the Master, teachers are especially fortunate. Jesus' chief business was teaching. Of all the ways that the Son of God could have chosen to unleash the Gospel message, He elected to be an itinerant educator. It is true that He was an evangelist. And Christ was known as a healer and a worker of miracles. Certainly He was a remarkable preacher. But a look at the biblical evidence reveals that the most far-reaching impact of Jesus' life and work came through His educational method.

The scriptural account of Jesus' life and ministry records numerous "teaching moments"—publicly in the synagogue, in the temple, and in the open air. In fact, Jesus is called "Teacher" more than any other title—forty-two times in the Gospel accounts. Another forty-seven times He is spoken of as "teaching." Christ apparently regarded Himself as a teacher. He never objected to being called by that name though there were other designations that He forbade both His followers and detractors to use. Everywhere He went Jesus responded to the cry "Master!"

Even those who disagreed with Him recognized Christ's identity as master and rabbi. Those Pharisees and Sadducees who opposed Jesus still called Him "the teacher." Nicodemus, himself a man of educational distinction and a member of the Sanhedrin, did not dare to publicly identify himself with Jesus' movement. Yet as a seeker approaching the Master he admitted, "Rabbi, we know You are a teacher" (John 3:2).

Perhaps the most powerful evidence for Jesus as educator is the entourage of disciples that accompanied Him. The disciples—literally "learners"—were a community of interested persons who saw in Jesus not only a speaker of memorable ability but also a model of righteous living. As a mentor, Jesus Christ opened up to these people not only His words, but His entire life. As with so many rabbis, the success or failure of the teacher was measured by what His pupils went on to accomplish. Certainly the results from Christ's tutelage of the disciples marks Him as one of the great—indeed the greatest—teachers of all time.

Succeeding generations, both believers and nonbelievers, have concurred. Historian Frederick Mayer asserts that "the impact of Jesus upon educational history . . . is enormous. His stamp can never be erased."[3] *Encyclopedia Judaica* agrees: "Even many persons who are not Christians believe that he was a great and wise teacher. He has probably influenced humanity more than anyone else who ever lived."[4] Listen to the first known Christian scholar, Clement of Alexandria: "Let us call Him by one title: Educator. . . "[5] It is generally agreed that, in the annals of history, Jesus is a teacher worthy of note. For the challenge of Christian education today, there is no better model. E. Stanley Jones is probably right: "In all the history of Christianity, whenever there has been a new emphasis upon Jesus, there has been a fresh outburst of spiritual vitality and virility."[6]

Jesus: the Teacher par excellence. That fact is clear. Some may accuse me of oversimplifying the goal of Christian education by suggesting that we should imitate the Master. I think not. It is true that with a different culture than that in which Jesus lived, and with increased technology, there may be some differences between our approach and His. My simple thesis is this: The objectives of Jesus still ring true for us today; His method is the most effective course—culture and technology notwithstanding. As we unfold His Master Plan, we will find it as relevant now as ever.

A monastery which flourished in the Middle Ages became known for a phrase with which the community began each day. The words were simple: "Let us begin again to be Christians."[7] Perhaps we should say much the same in our field of education today: "Let us begin again to be Christian—Christlike—educators." Those of us interested in pursuing that challenge must be willing to seek after the Leader and ask the question, "How did He do what He did?" That is the task at hand. The answer begins with why He did what He did— Jesus' educational objectives. It is with His goals that we begin our journey.

Beginning Steps . . .

1. *As you begin this study of Jesus as Teacher, write a prayer in the margin of this page committing yourself to follow His model. If you are in a group, join hands and make a corporate commitment to understand His style and employ it as completely as possible.*

2. *Based on Jesus' example, select an area of your teaching style in which you need to grow and identify several steps to take toward change. If using this book in a class setting, break up into groups of two or three to share and discuss your answers.*

3. *Choose one of the Gospel accounts and conduct your own in-depth Bible study of Jesus' teaching style. As you survey the book, note the who, what, why, when, where, and how of each educational encounter.*

4. *Recall one or two especially memorable teachers. What qualities made them outstanding or influential? Compare these attributes with Jesus' personality and educational approach, and identify specific qualities you could emulate.*

"George, Howard wasn't like us. Nobody ever
told him where he come from, and
so he didn't have an idea of
where he ought to be goin'."

—Kizzy
(in TV program "Roots," explaining
to her son why she cancelled
her impending wedding)

"You shall be to Me a kingdom of priests
and a holy nation."

—The God of Israel

The Three Objectives of Jesus:

◆ Disciples with holy character,
◆ Who act as priestly servants in His
world,
◆ And who constitute a faithful community
of relational believers.

CHAPTER TWO

THE OBJECTIVES
OF THE MASTER

It makes a difference if you know, and are excited about, where you are going. In the children's story *Winnie the Pooh,* for instance, Pooh and Piglet are out for an evening stroll before Piglet finally breaks the silence and asks, "When you wake up in the morning, Pooh, what's the first thing you say to yourself?"

"What's for breakfast?" answers Pooh. "And what do you say, Piglet?"

"I say, 'I wonder what exciting thing is going to happen today?' "[1]

There's a good lesson in those few lines for teachers. As teachers, we need to wake up in the morning reminding ourselves of the sustaining objectives we are shooting for, and what kind of exciting progress we are going to make toward those ends each day.

For a good instructor, that is the bottom line. Foundational to everything else are engaging, motivating, clear-cut, and well-defined objectives. Once you know where you are heading and are eager to get there, it's a lot easier to decide the means of the journey. But without any sense of inspiring direction we can—and often do—jump from program to program, activity to activity, while the results we desire continue to elude us. As people seeking to emulate Christ's educational example, our first task is to determine what He was trying to accomplish. Jesus had an agenda in mind when He launched His earthly ministry. And that agenda determined what He did, and when and why He did it. If we don't adopt the same objectives, we'll be off the track from the start.

Jesus was a Jew who came as the culmination of the salvation history God had initiated long years before with the Children of Israel. Christ didn't nullify God's original objectives for His people, but was the way to finally accomplish them. He came to make it possible for humans to be what God intended them to be, to do what He wanted them to do. And so the search for Jesus' objectives begins with a look backward in revelational history.

The Sinai Objectives

A watershed event in the history of Israel was her great deliverance from the bondage of slavery. In fact, the Book of Exodus that recounts this miraculous deliverance literally means "the way out" (Greek, *ex*-out + *hodos*-way). Similarly, our English word "educate" comes from the Latin *e* (out) + *ducere* (to lead)—a leading out. God, the Educator, had it in mind to lead the chosen people out of their predicament of bondage. But there was more. Good teachers don't just lead people away from ignorance and bondage; they enable their students to progress toward other worthwhile goals. Once the Israelites were out of Egypt, God intended to head them in the right direction.

In the nineteenth chapter of Exodus, the Lord brings His chosen people to the desert of Sinai and asks Moses to come up to the mountain so He can speak to the people through him. On the mountain, God tells Moses to remind the people of Israel of all that He has done for them. By grace He has delivered them. He has guided them out of their despicable, dehumanizing condition.

But the Educator wasn't finished. He declared that if the Israelites would obey Him, they would be a very special people indeed, for they would become a *kingdom of priests and a holy nation* (Ex. 19:6). In one of the most explicit and strategic statements in Scripture, God describes His objectives for the nation of Israel: (1) character reflective of her God (holy), (2) a service orientation to bring God's witness to the world (priests), and (3) a living and breathing community (plural!) of believers (kingdom, nation). This declaration and the momentous occurrences surrounding the Exodus/Sinai events were crucial for all of Israel's life and thought. For generations to come the Children of Israel would remember, if not always fulfill, these words.

Character

God's objectives highlighted the kind of people He wanted for His own—a holy nation. Holy is the quintessential description of God's own character. The more one surveys Scripture the more evident it becomes that holiness is not simply a divine attribute; rather, the word *holy* symbolizes that which is characteristic of God and corresponds precisely with His Person. When we speak of God as holy, we are talking about the very essence of who He is, His God-ness. Holy is a synonym for His deity.

Occasionally I bring this point up in a seminar or class and deliver the biblical case for it. Inevitably someone wonders, often aloud, "Hey, I thought God was love." This is true. God is many things. He is Love, He is Peace, He is Justice, and so forth. But when we speak in terms of God as such, we must recognize that each descriptor is qualified by His holiness. He is *holy* Love, *holy* Peace, and *holy* Justice.

Remember when Isaiah, the Old Testament prophet, and the Apostle John from the New Testament are given a glimpse of the eternal world? They see heavenly creatures singing praises. And what are they saying? They are not glorifying God with the sounds of "Love, love, love!" Instead, the sixth chapter of Isaiah and the fourth chapter of Revelation portray these celestial beings as worshipping God by singing, "Holy, holy, holy!" That word is descriptive of God and His unchangeable nature. As Revelation 4:8 proclaims, this is the Holy God—"who was, and is, and is to come!"

Dr. Dennis Kinlaw notes that our present understanding of

the word "holy" developed over a period of time.[2] Every culture, he suggests, differentiated the sacred from the secular in its vocabulary. The Canaanite people already possessed such religious terminology when Israel reached the Promised Land. What was sacred to the Canaanites, however, was disgusting in the eyes of the Lord. For instance, the temple prostitute was considered a holy woman; the homosexual priest, a holy man. Man's speech, not surprisingly, was as fallen as man himself!

In that pagan setting, the words for God and the sacred had to be filled with new content. The process, as Kinlaw points out, begins in Exodus 3:5. The ground upon which Moses stands is declared holy. Why? Because Jehovah is there. God begins to help the people understand that His presence is inseparable from holiness. From that point, many things are called holy—land, Jerusalem, the temple, the vessels used in its service, the persons who minister there, etc. The point is, whatever belongs to Jehovah is holy. Nothing is holy in and of itself, apart from God. Holy refers to that which is special because of the touch of God. Where His presence abides, there is holiness. Where He is absent, all is profane.

When the writers of the New Testament chose a word descriptive of God's essential being, they had five options: *hieros, hosios, semnos, hagios, hagnos.* They chose *hagios.* Why? Because *hagios* was, of the five terms, used least in Greek literature. It is never, for instance, found in Homer, Hesiod, or any of the Tragedians. Nowhere does it appear in Greek literature in reference to god or man. Evidently, the New Testament writers reasoned that since it was the least used, it was undoubtedly the least corrupted. The Holy God of Israel had again found vocabulary to describe His unique character.

Mark it well. Holy is the term that God has chosen to describe His essence—His nature. When He outlined His objectives for Israel, at Sinai, the Lord was essentially calling the people to be like Him. His overall and most powerful objective for us is that we reflect His image. To be sure, we cannot do so in every aspect. God is, for instance, omnipresent, omnipotent, omniscient. These terms basically mean that He tops the charts on presence, power, and knowledge. He is not limited in any way. The question should rightfully be asked, "How could we ever be like that?"

We can't. But we can reflect His moral attributes with the help of His Spirit. When God says to us, "You shall be holy, for I am holy" (Lev. 11:45), He is commanding that we optimize our finite faculties and abilities for Him. We do that by being like Him in very tangible ways. For instance, we learn what holy love is and we apply it, with the empowerment of His infilling, to our everyday living. We struggle together to understand His peace and become peacemakers in a world of strife. Justice is a vital theme in Scripture. Therefore, we learn of holy justice and practice it in our own lives. In short, to be holy is to let God's divine light shine into every nook and cranny of our lives, by His grace adjusting our priorities in obedience to His character.

One of my favorite short stories illustrates the process of redemptive change. Penned by Nathaniel Hawthorne, it is entitled "The Great Stone Face." The tale centers around a man named Ernest who grew up in a village renowned for a natural wonder that rested just outside its boundaries. Nature had majestically carved in the side of a mountain the features of a human visage so realistic that from a distance the Great Stone Face appeared to be alive.

The countenance was noble; the features, grand. Ernest, like all the children of the nearby village, was told of an ancient prophecy that at some future day a child would be born in the vicinity who would grow up to resemble the Stone Face. Upon learning that the promised prophet had not yet appeared, the young Ernest clapped his hands above his head and exclaimed, "I do hope that I shall live to see him!"

Ernest, growing older, never forgot that prophecy learned at his mother's knee. It was always on his mind. And as he grew to manhood, Ernest allowed the Great Stone Face to become his teacher—meditating upon the countenance, looking to it for solace, reading stories about it, speaking of it to those who would hear.

Years passed. Many came into the village claiming to be the promised one. But each time Ernest went out to meet the pretenders he came away crestfallen. For although these imposters claimed the honor, Ernest knew better. As a result of his devotion to the Face, he had become an expert on it. Surely Ernest, of all people, would know the one when he came. After each disappointment Ernest would return to the Face, peer into it and ask, "How long?" The granite features seemed to reassure him, "Fear not, Ernest, the man will come!"

Ernest was aged now, his hair gray and his gait slow. The one great sadness of his life was that he had never seen the prophet long foretold. One day a poet famous for his ode celebrating the Stone Face came to visit Ernest. They enjoyed each other's company, and yet each spoke sadly—for they longed to see the Face enfleshed.

The two talked long, and as the day drew to a close it came time for Ernest's daily discourse on the Great Stone Face. Each evening inhabitants of the neighboring village assembled in the open air for his stirring oration. There Ernest stood and spoke to the people, giving them what thoughts were in his heart and mind. Delivered with eloquence, the words were powerful because they matched his character and harmonized beautifully with his life of devotion.

The poet, as he listened, grew teary-eyed. Ernest's words were nobler by far than any poetry he had ever written. Struck by the grandeur of the moment, and with the Great Stone Face looming in the background, the poet suddenly realized what should have been obvious all along. For Ernest, he noticed, had a mild, sweet, beautiful countenance that looked like the Stone Face itself!

Moved by an irresistible impulse, the poet threw his arms aloft and began to shout to all who would hear—"Behold, behold! Ernest is himself the likeness of the Great Stone Face!" And with that all the people sitting about looked at Ernest and noticed that what the poet said was true. The prophecy was fulfilled! Ernest had become like his ideal.

Hawthorne's story packs a powerful punch. It recognizes a

simple truth: What gets our attention gets us. The Lord God of Israel wanted to move into the lives of the Hebrew people in a powerful, holy way. He desired that they fix their attention upon Him—let this one God become their Teacher and the focus of their adoration and worship. To that end, the Lord instructed His people to speak of Him in their households, as they walked along the byways, as they lay down to sleep, and as they rose to work. If they followed that pattern, then like Hawthorne's Ernest they would develop, by His grace and not just their efforts, God-like attributes and a noble character. An obedient Israel could be holy—even as her Redeemer was holy.

The Holy Educator—God Almighty—worked with and through the Israelites and then became holiness incarnate in the person of Jesus the Teacher, who in turn sent the Holy Spirit. And for what reason? To help us attain to the loftiest of all objectives—holy lives marked by godly character.

Service

If the first and foremost of God's objectives for His people is holy character, then another quickly follows. From character springs action. God declared that Israel should be a kingdom of priests. When He established the priesthood in Israel, the priest was essentially God's representative. He was an agent of outreach and service. Priests were to serve God by devotion to Him and obedience in every phase of life. But they also served man as they bore God's message. In essence, they stood between God and man and acted as mediators— drawing the two parties together. In order to do that, it was essential that the priests maintain right relations with both men and their Maker.

The priests of Israel and God's instructions for them represented, in many ways, what God wanted for all of Israel. They were to set by precept and example a godly standard of character and purity, proper conduct in relation to God, and special concern for those less fortunate. In Israel, the priests were most capable of protecting the unfortunate from oppression, strengthening the moral conscience of their nation, affecting public policy, and educating their society. Their importance for the development of holy living, justice concerns, and societal morality cannot be overestimated.

The emphasis upon service for all of Israel is clearly seen in Leviticus. They are first commanded to be holy like God (19:2), which presumes a right relationship with their Creator and Sustainer. Then, in the verses following this command, the injunction is particularized in terms of service to their fellow man. Holy character was to be demonstrated by such actions as the provision of gleaning for the poor and the sojourner; prohibitions against oppression of neighbors, servants, and the handicapped; injunctions for ethical dealings with fellow men; various commands meant for justice which included respect for the aged, love for the stranger, and other forms of social action.

God never intended for character to exist in a vacuum. He made it clear through the priests that holiness and service cannot be divorced. Israel was called to be holy, and God filled that calling with specific content in terms of lifestyle. The Israelites were to be His mediators to the world. They were called to cultivate godly character and upright action. Godliness, as reflected in His people, belongs in humble, loving, overflowing ministry.

To demonstrate this point in my classes, I often choose an unsuspecting student and coax him into holding a glass full of water. I make the "volunteer" promise not to spill the water under any circumstances. Since that appears to be a simple enough task, the student invariably agrees. Then, very slowly and deliberately, I seize his arm and shake it. Water goes everywhere—on him, on me, on the floor, and sometimes on the unfortunate folks who sit in the front row. When asked why he allowed the water to spill, you can bet that "You shook my arm!" is the predictable—and incorrect response. "Water did not come out of the glass because I shook his arm," I will say. "Water came out of the glass because there was water in the glass."

An old proverb says: Whatever you're filled to the brim with will spill out when you are bumped. So it is with holy character. If we are filled to the brim with the Spirit of God and reflect His moral character, when needs and situations in the world "bump" us, we will spill out with the kind of priestly actions that are pleasing to Him.

Community

The final objective of God for His people might be overlooked without careful observation. Notice that God calls for a "kingdom" of priests and a holy "nation." These terms suggest corporate commitment which transcends a mere individual faith. God's conditional challenge at Sinai treated this responsibility to one another and to Himself not merely as a means to an end but an end in itself.

The foundation of Israel's religion rests in the well-known words of Deuteronomy 6: "Hear O Israel: The Lord is our God, the Lord is one." While the pagan cultures surrounding Israel worshiped multiple gods, Israel was notable for her strict monotheism. With the New Testament and the church's understanding of the Trinity, we maintain that within that unity there is a plurality. Three Persons make up the Trinity — Father, Son, and Holy Spirit. This is significant, because just as the God of Israel was three Persons in one Being, He desires His people to reflect Him as individuals within a unified Body. God wanted His people (plural) in community (unity) because He is Community — Three in One. Intimacy among God's people is a reflection of Him.

This strategy of community among the faithful is necessary for, as social scientists remind us, no distinctive and dissonant identity can be long maintained without the support of a group. Peter Berger describes the Jewish community this way. He says:

> [it is difficult to maintain] a supernaturalist position in the teeth of a cognitively antagonistic world. . . . Unless our theologian has the inner fortitude of a desert saint, he has only one effective remedy against the threat of cognitive collapse in the face of these pressures. He must huddle together with like-minded deviants — and huddle very

closely indeed. Only in a counter community of considerable strength does cognitive deviance have a chance to
maintain itself. *The countercommunity provides continuing
therapy against the creeping doubt as to whether, after all,
one may not be wrong and the majority right. . . . In sum,
it must be a kind of ghetto.*[3] *[emphasis mine]*

A ghetto? You bet. In fact, Berger maintains that the Jews
created the ghetto out of religious necessity. Ghetto literally
means a part of the city where a distinctive people-group lives.
In these cloisters the group constitutes a cluster of "like-minded deviants," to use Berger's terminology. Deviant, quite
apart from any negative connotation, in this case denotes a
people who think and act differently from society's norms—in
essence, have a distinctive culture, as did the people of Israel.
If deviants of this sort are to survive in the world, says
Berger, they must huddle together very closely.

I heard one scholar suggest that a contemporary Jew can
live in a Gentile world all day long, fifty-two weeks out of the
year, if that Jew can return home at night to a Jewish wife, his
beautiful Jewish children and kosher food, and pray to the one
God of Israel. He can survive, if he can gather with his "like-
minded deviants." The same is true for the Christian. We can
live out the high calling of God in a fallen world, but not as lone
rangers. To stay true to Christ, we need the fellowship, encouragement, and exhortation of other believers.

Why the need for community? Because holy character and
priestly service are never found without it. We will stick to our
commitments much more faithfully when there are others of
like mind who are willing to encourage us, exhort us, and hold
us accountable to our calling. And saints of every age have
found this to be true. John Wesley said it well. "Christianity is
a social religion," he proclaimed, "and to turn it into a solitary
religion is to destroy it. I do not mean that it cannot subsist so
well, but that it cannot subsist at all, without society; without
living and conversing with other men."[4] Character, service,
and community are a package deal. They always have been—
the Educator tells us in Exodus—right from the beginning.

Toward the Jesus Synthesis

The biblical record not only supports these three powerful objectives of God for Israel, but it also shows their adoption by Jesus for His own course of education. The parallel is evident in the Sermon on the Mount. In this passage lies the manifesto of His message. Matthew, recording a short history of Jesus' life, is well-known as the writer to the Jews. In fact, some have suggested that the former tax collector was attempting to create a "New Testament Pentateuch" by an arrangement which contains elements similar to those in the first five books of the Bible. One case in point is the five major discourses in Matthew's Gospel. Each one of the supposed divisions concludes with the same formula: "When Jesus had finished these sayings . . ." (7:28; 11:1; 13:53; 19:1; 26:1, RSV) There are five books in the Jewish Torah and five major discourses in the Gospel written to the Jews. With such an outline posited, it is little wonder that some scholars call the Sermon on the Mount, "The Sinai of the New Testament."

For instance, just as Moses went up on the mountain to receive the Old Covenant, Jesus ascended the Mount to give His followers the working stuff of their faith. The first words He utters are a set of statements, known as the Beatitudes, which issue a clear call to character. These brief statements have been called the sum of all true religion by some and Jesus' self portrait by others. Jesus was suggesting to His company what they should "be" as members of the Kingdom.

As God at Sinai reminded the Israelites, however, it is quite clear that the Redeemer wants the character of His disciples to bear fruit in action. Jesus moved quickly from the Beatitudes to remind His listeners that they were to be "salt" and "light" unto the world. He admonished them to live as godly examples and do good works for all to see. They were to let their holiness flow into the world, impacting their environment for God. And, as the passage suggests, the entire message was given in the context of a community of disciples. Essentially, the chapters which follow are in both instances exposition on the practical implications of living under God's authority, cultivating a vibrant faith, meeting the challenge of upright living, and maintaining proper relationships with one's fellow man.

The Sermon on the Mount is merely a window by which one can take a panoramic view of the totality of Jesus' ministry. The distinctives of Jesus' message stated there are evident throughout His work and proclamations elsewhere in Scripture. But I find this particular passage a powerful reminder to us of how we should *be, do,* and *relate* as Christian people. The Sermon on the Mount has had such an impact on my life that I have memorized it. Occasionally I deliver the Sermon in dramatized form for congregations. Afterward someone usually approaches me with a comment like, "Boy, Jesus sure lays it on the line in that one, doesn't He?" He certainly does, and with three overarching objectives in mind.

A common proverb needles us with the reminder that "He who aims at nothing, hits it." Objectives and goals, in other words, are important. In *Alice in Wonderland,* Alice encountered the Cheshire Cat. " 'Would you tell me please, which way I ought to go from here?' she asked the cat. 'That depends a good deal on where you want to get to,' said the Cheshire Cat. 'I don't much care where . . . ' said Alice. 'Then it doesn't matter which way you go,' said the Cat."

It can never be said that the Educator didn't know where He wanted His students to go. It is quite clear that He desired a people like Himself, whose character and actions and relationships with each other reflected Him. To those who had been with Him and seen Him in action, "to be like" this God was definitely a goal to get excited about in the morning.

Jesus was a teacher. And, like the God of Israel, He had definite goals in mind. But how did He meet them? Keep reading to find out.

Beginning Steps . . .

1. Define the objectives discussed in this chapter—character, service, and community—in terms of the context in which you teach. What do they mean for you and your students? What can you begin doing to help your students more accurately reflect

God's intention for us? Put it in writing!

2. *List these objectives in three columns at the top of a blank sheet of paper. Now take your Sunday School quarterly, Bible study guide, or other teaching material and evaluate an upcoming lesson, listing the planned information and activities under the appropriate headings. How balanced is the lesson?*

3. *Brainstorm ways to supplement the weakest area from above. Be creative! (It helps to have a group for this beginning step!)*

Go to the people, live among them,
Learn from them, love them.
Start with what they know,
Build on what they have.

—a Chinese poem

The Lord Himself will give you a sign: Behold
a virgin will be with child and bear a son,
and she will call His name Immanuel.

—Isaiah, son of Amoz

Incarnational Teachers . . .

- ▶ Identify with those whom they want to teach and communicate,
- ▶ Pose themselves as sensitive learners,
- ▶ Embody the message they want to perpetuate.

CHAPTER THREE

EDUCATION AS INCARNATION: IDENTIFYING, LEARNING, EMBODYING

The Rev. Keith Tonkel of Wells United Methodist Church in Jackson, Mississippi decided to start off his Wednesday evening service with a group exercise. "If I could take every religious word away from you except one, what would it be?" he proposed. The members of Wells Church had grown used to such interesting challenges from their pastor, and they could be counted on to come up with insightful responses. After mulling it over for a few short moments, the small crowd began to respond. "I guess I would take the word 'love,' " one of the youth thoughtfully ventured. Another young man chose "faith." The folks gathered there nodded their heads in approval. Others suggested "salvation" and "hope." Good choices all. One elderly lady thought "Christ" was the best of all possibilities. "Of course! Christ!" a Sunday School teacher whispered under her breath to a friend. "Why didn't I think of that?"

While these responses were being tried on for size, Pastor Keith noticed an interesting dynamic taking place in the back of the sanctuary. "Uncle Matt" Dukes, sitting staunchly on the back row of oak pews, was shaking his head back and forth with each of the proffered responses and vehemently muttering "No, no," after each suggestion. The youth, sitting near him, began to snicker and roll their eyes in mock embarrassment but Matt continued his naysaying. He obviously considered his the "best" answer, and nothing less would do. Keith called on all who wanted to try their hand at the congregational exercise, purposely saving Matt until last. After everyone else had made a contribution, the pastor finally said, "Uncle Matt, it looks as if you have a word."

"I certainly do," was the ready reply.

"Well, what is it?"

"My word is the best!" he confidently asserted. "And if you want to know where to find it, it's in the Gospel according to St. Matthew, chapter one and verse twenty-three. There you will read, 'They shall call His name Immanuel.' My word," he boldly stated, "is Immanuel." Most of those sitting around Uncle Matt that evening, primed for the "word to end all words," responded with confusion: "Immanuel? What in the world is he talking about?"

"Yes," said Matt as he continued undaunted, "Immanuel means 'God with us.' " The congregation, suddenly more impressed, turned toward this saint for further explanation. "You see," he explained, "if God is with us we have faith, we have hope, we have love, and salvation—all the words said here tonight. And yes, we even have Christ." The old man cracked a smile before adding his last punch, "You see, I told you I had the best word."

The Principle of Identification

To be among His people has always been God's desire. This theme, running throughout Scripture, is particularly evident at Mount Sinai where He proclaimed, "I will meet . . . with the sons of Israel . . . I will consecrate the tent of meeting . . . and I will dwell among the sons of Israel and will be their God" (Ex. 29:43-45). It was the intention of the Hebrew God to dwell among His chosen people, to be in their midst. He instructed them how to construct a portable sanctuary—called the Tabernacle—which was to be the place of meeting where Israel could interact with her God.

It is fascinating then, that in the prologue to his Gospel, John points out, "The Word became flesh and dwelt among us"

(1:14). Notice the significance of these few words. The enfleshed Word—the Incarnation, is the God who desires to be close to His people—the One who dwells among us. The Greek word for dwelt (*eskēnōsen*) translates as "tabernacled." In other words, when God came in the form of a man, He "tabernacled" or "pitched a tent" in our midst—a clear parallel to His activity in Exodus. Jehovah on the mountaintop of Sinai is the Lord of the New Testament—same God, same purpose. He wants to identify. He wants to be with us. His intention is "up close" proximity.

The teacher desiring to emulate Jesus' teaching style will pay close attention to this principle of identification. Jesus "pitched a tent" in Palestine to reach a few people who in turn would turn the world upside down for His Kingdom. He identified with the Jewish people of that dusty colony in several ways: through their environment, religion, political struggles, occupations, economy, sorrows, and joys. Even His name—Jesus—was a very common one among the Jews of that day. He was one of them. Such empathy was crucial to His ultimate effectiveness. Says one of my professorial colleagues, "My guess is that when Jesus started speaking, He understood His audience for He had been with them. Therefore, when He spoke to them, they heard—they really heard."

There are examples today of people who practice identification, seeking to empathize with the plight of others. For instance, John Howard Griffin was a white man who studied racism in the United States by darkening his skin with dye and a chemical and then traveling as a black man in the South. Out of his experiences he wrote the book *Black Like Me*, undoubtedly one of the most penetrating and practical understandings of what it was like to suffer racism in the white-dominated world of the 1960s. Recently, several young individuals have been in the news for going undercover by taking on the guise of the elderly to investigate the treatment of the aged in America. One of my friends in graduate school spent his spring break as a "street person" in a nearby metropolitan area. The stories he brought back were chilling, to say the least. In each of these cases, people gained a kind of insight and understanding possible only through intentional incarnation. They became physically and emotionally involved in a problem and as a result developed a deep-set empathy. Through such intellectual and emotional identification mere talkers are transformed into activists, communicators, and life-changing educators.

Compassion that identifies with others reminds me of that day in Caesarea Philippi when Jesus turned to the disciples and asked them, " 'Who do people say that the Son of Man is?' " And they said, 'Some say John the Baptist; some, Elijah, and others, Jeremiah' " (Matt. 16:13-14). Why Jeremiah? Here was a prophet who never performed a miracle, did not experience even the faintest moment of triumph, or win a single convert. No one was moved by his message and he died in Egypt among a people unwilling to repent. What did Jesus — miracle worker, eloquent preacher, insightful teacher, soul-winner — have in common with him? Some scholars suggest that the cause of this "mistaken identity" lies in the fact that Jeremiah personally and compassionately identified with the sufferings and heartaches of his people. While this prophet knew little success as we are apt to define it, he personally cared for and identified with his people, so much so that when Christ appeared the disciples couldn't help but be reminded of him. Would that we could all be mistaken for such a one as Jeremiah! Jesus was successful because He dared to intentionally identify with the people He sought to influence.[1]

Like Jesus and Jeremiah, it is important for us as teachers to identify without getting completely absorbed. There is a difference between identification and accommodation. Both men, for instance, were very much a part of the worlds in which they lived. Yet they also posed a striking contrast to the society around them. This "in but not of" quality is particularly evident in the life of Jesus. He "emptied Himself, taking the form of a bond-servant . . . being made in the likeness of men" (Phil. 2:7). He did so to present an example of a new order.

In the late second century *Letter to Diognetus*, the writer portrays the same kind of tension in describing the Christians. They were a part of their world, explains the *Letter*, yet vastly different from it.

Christians cannot be distinguished from the rest of mankind by country, speech, or customs. They do not live in cities of their own; they do not speak a special language; they do not follow a peculiar manner of life. . . . *They conform to the customs of their country in dress, food, and the general mode of life, and yet they show a remarkable, an admittedly extraordinary structure of their own life together. They live in their own countries, but only as guests and aliens. They take part in everything as citizens and endure everything as aliens. Every foreign country is their homeland, and every homeland is a foreign country to them.* . . . *In a word: what the soul is in the body, the Christians are in the world. As the soul is present in all the members of the body, so Christians are present in all the cities of the world. As the soul lives in the body, yet does not have its origin in the body, so the Christians live in the world yet are not of the world.*[2] *(emphasis mine)*

There is incredible power in this lesson: alike, yet different. Lawrence of Arabia once said that "No man would lead the Arabs except he ate the rank's food, wore their clothes, lived level with them, and yet appeared better in himself."[3] Similarly one of the vital lessons of identification, and a definite challenge for the teacher as an "incarnate one," is that we must be change agents without a shift in our foundational Christlike emphasis.

One way that identification enhances understanding and communication is by allowing the communicator the crucial experience of getting into the mainstream of a mindset. In recent years I have enjoyed reading *The Cotton Patch Gospels*. They were assembled by Clarence Jordan who in the 1960's founded Koinonia Farms, a pioneering interracial farming community in Americus, Georgia. Jordan, who earned the Ph.D. in New Testament Greek, immersed himself in the original language of the New Testament and then translated the Scriptures into terminology that could be understood by the people with whom he lived and worked. Throughout the Gospel story, Dr. Jordan attempted to strip away the fancy language and the barriers of time and distance by putting Jesus and other biblical figures in the midst of the modern world of the Deep South in which he lived. In so doing, he placed the arrival of Jesus not in Bethlehem, but in Gainesville, Georgia. Jerusalem becomes Atlanta; Rome is Washington, D.C. Christ's inner circle of disciples consists of Rock (Peter), Jim (James), and Jack (John). The Pharisees are portrayed as upstanding church members and the scribes as theologians and seminary professors.

While Jordan found this new interpretation risky and was painfully aware of the limitations and imperfections of his efforts, he nonetheless did a delightful job of making comparisons and matching biblical people, groups, and settings with modern counterparts. His translation of The Good Samaritan is a highlight. I want you to notice the words in brackets, which were part of Jordan's footnotes. He includes these not as an actual translation gained from the analysis of the original Greek but as probabilities of thought.

The story begins as the teacher of the adult Sunday School class asks, "Just who is my neighbor?"

Then Jesus laid into him and said, "A man was going from Atlanta to Albany and some gangsters held him up. When they had robbed him of his wallet and brand-new suit, they beat him up and drove off in his car, leaving him unconscious on the shoulder of the highway.

"Now it just so happened that a white preacher was going down the same highway. When he saw the fellow, he stepped on the gas and went scooting by. [His homiletical mind probably made the following outline: 1. I do not know the man. 2. I do not wish to get involved in any court proceedings. 3. I don't want to get blood on my new upholstering. 4. The man's lack of proper clothing would embarrass me upon my arrival in town. 5. And finally, brethren, a minister must never be late for worship services.] Shortly afterward, a white Gospel song leader came down the road, and when he saw what had happened he too stepped on the gas. [What his thoughts were we'll never know, but as he

whizzed past, he may have been whistling, 'Brighten the corner, where you are.']

"Then a black man traveling that way came upon the fellow, and what he saw moved him to tears. He stopped and bound up his wounds as best he could, drew some water from his water-jug to wipe away the blood and then laid him on the back seat. [All the while his thoughts may have been along this line: 'Somebody's robbed you; yeah, I know about that, I been robbed, too. And they done beat you up bad; I know, I been beat up, too. And everybody just go right on by and leave you laying here hurting. Yeah, I know. They pass me by, too.'] He drove on into Albany and took him to the hospital and said to the nurse, 'You take good care of this white man I found on the highway. Here's the only two dollars I got, but you all keep account of what he owes, and if he can't pay it, I'll settle up with you when I make a pay-day.'

"Now if you had been the man held up by the gangsters, which of these three—the white preacher, the white song leader, or the black man—would you consider to have been your neighbor?"

The teacher of the adult Bible class said, "Why, of course, the nig—I mean, er ... well, er ... the one who treated me kindly."

Jesus said, "Well, then, you get going and start living like that!"[4]

Clarence Jordan, working in Georgia in the 1950s and 1960s, communicated the story of the Good Samaritan in language understood by a community that, like the Jews and the Samaritans, knew racial tension. As did the parables in Jesus' day and age, *The Cotton Patch Gospels* come across in contemporary America with a certain bite that speaks to the pious and the heathen, rich and poor, black and white. How was Jordan able to do it? He had lived among blacks in the Civil Rights era South—become incarnate within their culture—and came to understand how Jesus might have told the story in that cultural milieu. He was immersed in the Word and immersed in his society—a methodology modeled in word and example by the Rabbi Jesus. And note who stopped to pick up the man on the edge of the highway: the one who could *identify* with what it felt like to be robbed, beaten up, and ignored. The lesson is clear: physically and emotionally identifying with the situations of others enables us to communicate more effectively.

Contemporary teachers need to take note: Putting ourselves in somebody else's shoes, seeing life through their eyes, and experiencing their joys and sorrows—all allow us to gain an absolutely invaluable perspective for education. With that knowledge we can tailor our message to match their readiness and meet their needs. Our empathy will more than likely open avenues for the penetration of the Good News.

Assuming the Position of Learner

God did not have to come as a babe wrapped in swaddling clothes. Conceivably, He could have burst on the scene in any form or fashion—even as a full-grown, bearded thirty-year-old itinerant rabbi. But He chose instead to enter the world like everybody else and to grow up slowly, waiting, praying, and studying for thirty years before beginning His ministry. In the biblical accounts, one of the most striking aspects of the Incarnation is that Jesus posited Himself as a learner, someone who needed to grow in "wisdom and stature, and in favor with God and men" (Luke 2:52).

While Scripture gives little explicit detail about Jesus' childhood and youth, the life and words of the man we meet in the Gospels at least hint at several truths. As a boy growing up in Palestine, He most likely had several teachers. We may surmise that Jesus was raised in a devout Jewish home, and as such Joseph, the father, was charged with the responsibility of carrying out the instructions of the Shema—to diligently teach the tenets of the faith to his children in rising and retiring. So the man Joseph, who served as the earthly father of Jesus, was His teacher. Jesus also learned from nature. The wealth of parabolic material contained in the Gospels points out His keen awareness of the world around Him and His ability to illustrate spiritual principles with examples from the plant and animal kingdoms.

It is probable that Jesus received some type of formal religious instruction, a common practice among Jewish boys past and present. While this is conjecture, the results of His training are evident. Luke 2:41-47 records His encounter, as a youth of twelve, with the teachers in the Temple courts. His parents, having lost track of Jesus during the Passover festivities in Jerusalem, found Him "sitting in the midst of the teachers, both listening to them, and asking them questions." Already the posture of the learner and the thirst to know and understand was in place. "And all who heard Him were amazed at His understanding and His answers." Jesus' thorough acquaintance with Scripture comes across vividly in the Gospel accounts, where He quotes extensively from the Old Testament and explains its teachings with clarity, insight, and authority that amazed His listeners. God Himself, come as man, took on the attitude of a listener, a learner, and a student of Scripture so that He might communicate the truth He embodied in words and actions that they could understand.

It should be no secret that great teaching and learning are so intertwined as to be virtually inseparable. For instance, the Hebrew words for teach (*lamad*) and learn (*limmud*) both derive from the same root *l-m-d*. It helps communicate the fact that an outstanding teacher must be a diligent learner; the excellent learner has the best opportunity to be a great teacher. The concepts are necessarily woven together in the life and career of the Master. Teaching and learning are part and parcel of the same package of communication.

The best teachers and leaders generally do assume this "learner stance." I remember the evening when one of my professors, perched on his desk, made what he evidently considered a bold and thought-provoking declaration. "The end of all knowledge," he stated expansively, "is ignorance—a questioning mind!" His lesson was simple: to be educated was to be a person in continuous thirst of knowledge, a lifelong learner. But when he made his statement I know what he thought would happen. We students were undoubtedly supposed to hesitate, ponder his statement, and then murmur to ourselves something about its penetrating profundity. No such luck. Instead, one of my colleagues immediately blurted out, "I wish we had known about that objective before we forked over all this money for tuition!" The professor wasn't ready for what followed. Within seconds of his lofty pronouncement we were all doubled over in uproarious laughter. We meant no irreverence; as broke and overworked (or so we thought) university students, we were simply enjoying a moment of comic relief. Our professor, predictably, wasn't laughing, or smiling, or even slightly amused. But to his credit he made a quick and memorable rejoinder. In the midst of our laughter, he peered at the source of that untimely remark and replied simply, "Oh really? I would pay a lot for that kind of education, and so would have Socrates!"

Learning: It Pays to Be Attuned

Michelangelo's favorite motto was *Ancora Imparo*—"I am still learning."[5] In those few words, he articulated an important element of education recognized by most great teachers and communicators. Neil Postman has said that too often children enter schools as question marks only to leave as periods. If true, what a sad commentary this is on education in public, private, or church schools. We must learn to cultivate "the question mark" in our children—in students of any age. We need to develop ourselves as "question marks" where the Lord has placed us—to repeatedly ask relevant questions, sympathetically listen to the answers, and then step in to address the needs we discover. That is what great teaching is all about.

While effectiveness in communication demands that we learn this lesson, too often we are slow to pick up on it. Several years ago I asked an anthropologist friend, who happens to be a committed Christian, why it was that so many of those we knew on the mission field appeared to be ineffective. As a former missionary he had a great deal to say, and his insights were profound. I've never forgotten the following message that he relayed to me during our interview. He said, "Matt,

we have far too high an opinion of ourselves."
"How often do we go consciously expecting to learn? We don't. We go as the teachers and as the authorities. If we go as theologians, we've been trained with all the right doctrine; if we go as doctors, we've been trained with all the right surgical techniques. If agriculturalists, we go with all the right grains of river rice to grow. . . . It creates an endless mentality of the expert. I find that people learn and will be more open to what you have to say if you take the posture of a learner and fellow pilgrim."[6]

I have found that advice to be pertinent and useful in my own career. People are much more responsive if they know that I care enough about them to probe, listen, and learn. The minute they sense that I want them to shut up so I can voice my opinions, I have hampered genuine communication. They might politely listen, but I can really expect little more than that. The best way to reach a people group, at home or abroad, is to train oneself for employment in a targeted field and geographic location and then become an agent of change through physical, emotional, economical, and spiritual involvement with that people. That is true involvement, real incarnation, effective identification. When people recognize that you are attempting to listen and understand them by becoming like one of them, they are more likely to respond positively to your message. The Greek word for ministry in the New Testament expresses this concept. It is *diakonia*—through (*dia*) the dust (*konia*). If we desire to love, communicate, serve, and teach we must go "through the dust" (which made a lot of sense in ancient Palestine) with those to whom we desire to relay our life-changing message.

But to be effective, assuming the learner position can't be merely a communication gimmick, we must do so out of a genuine desire to learn and understand. At the campus of Texas Tech in Lubbock, Texas you will find a group called the Wesley Foundation. They have a program bubbling with excitement as young people engage in Bible study, social action, evangelism, dialogue with Christian leaders from across the nation, and fellowship—mixed in with large doses of fun.

But the Wesley Foundation at Texas Tech was not always so dynamic. Before director Steve Moore came, it consisted of a handful of individuals wondering how to resurrect a faltering campus ministry. Moore huddled with the small group and together they began to ask some serious questions:

1. *What are the needs of the people of this campus?*

2. *Where are these folks spiritually, intellectually, and emotionally?*

3. *What is the message we really desire to communicate?*

4. *What is the most effective way to communicate our message as good news and not bad/irrelevant news?*

5. *What will this good news mean in terms of behavior, values, and world view to people in this setting?*

6. *How can we unlock the university mindset to our message?*

Armed with the right questions this small group began to gather and analyze the answers. Then they took the bold but needed steps to structure their basic program to meet the many needs of the Texas Tech community. Today the outreach of this campus organization is one of the bright spots of ministry anywhere in the country. The Texas Tech Wesley Foundation now involves on a regular basis some eight hundred people per week. The secret? They courageously took the position of listening, inquiring learners, asking the right questions and humbly being taught by the answers. They identified those to whom they desired to minister and found out what made those people tick. They structured a program to meet genuine, researched needs. They allowed their approach to change, grow, and adapt along the way to meet those needs. Steve Moore is a teacher who captured the Spirit of Jesus, in large measure, because he dared to learn and to equip others to do the same, and to make the acquired answers count for the kingdom.

It is not really a unique testimony. Wherever successful educational ministry flourishes you will most likely find, at the helm, a communicator with a burning passion to learn and grow. That leader will want to learn more about Scripture, about his culture, and about how he can effectively take the message he loves to the people who need it most. And best of all, this person on the cutting edge of ministry will equip others for the same kind of redemptive inquiry and activity. A movement powered by such people is difficult to contain.

In classes or seminars, I am invariably challenged on this "incarnation as learning" idea. The typical line goes something like this: "I already know what people need. They need a personal relationship with Jesus and the pure milk of the Word!" That attitude reminds me of an unfortunate incident from the history of missions. A young German Lutheran named Bartholomaus Ziegenbalg worked as a pioneer missionary in South India early in the 18th century. Before beginning to communicate his message of the Good News he first attempted to master the Tamil language, understand Hindu religious beliefs and customs, and thoroughly comprehend and analyze the culture. His diligent labor resulted in a lengthy and insightful manuscript on Indian culture and religious belief. The quick response of mission executives was to put it on the shelf and rebuke Ziegenbalg for wasting his time. He had not been sent to write insightful manuscripts, but to preach the Gospel![7]

It is true; people need a personal relationship with Jesus and the pure milk of the Word. In that sense, basic needs are alike. In another sense, however, there are as many different needs as there are cultures, languages, tribes, churches, families, and individuals. And it may take some work to discover what they are. This was poignantly pointed out by my anthropologist friend, "Let's talk in terms of culture," he said and went on:

We should never assume that all needs are alike. Sometimes, what we think are needs may already be met. For

THE MASTER PLAN OF TEACHING

instance, in American society, people go off to one place for work, to another place for worship, one for market, one for banking, and still another for school—these are what we call simplex roles. Simplex roles are one strand relationships. You're in one context, and that's the only context that I see you in. The result is shallow relationships and nameless people in our lives. To talk about Jesus as Friend, for instance, makes a lot of sense.

But in a multiplex society, you don't have the problem of alienation and loneliness. Clans are huddled together; extended families are crowded under one roof. Every relative you have may be within a three mile radius. To talk about Jesus as Friend in a multiplex society doesn't make sense at all. People want to talk about Jesus as Protector, as a Sustainer of life, as Life itself. But Jesus as Friend? "I don't have any sense of loneliness! I've got too many friends/companions/relatives as it is!" they are likely to say. Understanding these and a multitude of other dynamics will make a radical difference in terms of the context of your ministry.[8]

Missionaries and ministers are used to taking this contextual approach with the written Word. A standard seminary course is biblical exegesis, which enables students to critically interpret a text or portion of Scripture for effective teaching and preaching. They analyze the linguistic and grammatical elements of a Scripture passage and attempt to determine its meaning. Using such training, Bible translators often have to make interesting allowances for cultural differences. John Jefferson Davis informs us that a number of African languages have no word for snow. If one stops to think about it, why should they? So translators have found it helpful to change the "white as snow" language of Scripture to something that communicates within those African cultures. The solution: "white as egret feathers!"—not a literal translation, but a cultural equivalent.[9]

The argument here is for cultural exegesis, critically examining and interpreting a society, people group, or person to understand and meet the needs of their lives. Teachers who succeed in communicating their message have discovered how such learning takes place and implement the necessary measures to target truth where their students are. Some of us just happen upon the right method; most of us have to work hard at asking good questions of and about our people and then seeking ways to meet their needs. All students need special attention paid to their background and current situations. I heard of a teacher recently who took his outline into a bar every Saturday night and asked the question, "What difference does this stuff make to them?" This is relevance via critical analysis. It pays to be attuned.

Quite simply, we must know the people with whom we desire to communicate. As we gain insight into their lives—what they know, feel, say, believe, and do—we are better able to express our love, care, and message to them in appropriate and responsible ways. Understanding these realities will certainly enhance our ministry to a group of people, whether they be around the block or around the world. I am always saddened by pastors and teachers who think that what their audience really needs is a more clever speech or well-delivered lesson plan. While these are helpful tools, such an approach is too one-dimensional to be effective in the long run. If Jesus took thirty years in intimate identification and in study of Scripture, His culture, and the needs of His people, shouldn't we modern teachers and communicators spend significant time—hours, days, months, years—in a similar search for understanding? The man or woman of action may argue that the days are so critical that we don't have that kind of time. The fact of the matter is, we don't have enough time not to. We can understand, recognize, and meet needs only as we take time to get to know the people they represent. For effective education, incarnation is not an option, it's essential.

Embody Your Message
Of course, coming "in the flesh" as an educator means that your most powerful medium of influence is the testimony of your life. When Jesus chose the teaching profession as His

mode of outreach He stood, in many ways, in a long line of rabbinic tradition which undoubtedly influenced His instructional activity. It was common procedure for a rabbi to associate closely with his pupils and teach them the great lessons of Scripture and tradition. Such close contact afforded the student the opportunity to "see"—in the character, service, and relationships of the rabbi what was being "said." The words of the rabbi were precious, his example, more precious still.

It is clear that this dynamic was present in the Master's relationship with His followers, the Twelve in particular. During their time of apprenticeship with Jesus, He modeled before them both actions and attitudes. From the outset, Jesus called His disciples to a lifestyle characterized by spiritual devotion.

But Jesus did more than tell others what to do; He caused them to hunger for the righteousness they needed by demonstrating, in His own life, a vital relationship with the Father. The Twelve knew of the times when He slipped away for communion with God. They observed close up His consistency over a period of time. And one day they approached Jesus and begged, "Lord, teach us to pray!" (Luke 11:1) What a teachable moment! Jesus didn't set them down at the outset and deliver a systematic discourse on prayer. No, He told them it was important, and then spent more time doing than talking. And His modeling created readiness for further instruction on the subject.

The same could be said for His knowledge of Scripture. Jesus' followers were with Him all the time. They were present when the scribes and Pharisees challenged Jesus and saw the way He quieted their arguments. The disciples frequently heard Him quote from the Scripture. At some point He must have recounted to them His temptation—one of the few events recorded in the Gospels at which none of them would have been present—and demonstrated the power of the Word to counter Satan's attacks. Perhaps up until that time not all of the disciples were as interested in knowing God's Word as they could have been.

It's easy to imagine a rough and ready fisherman like Peter being more concerned about getting to work on the boats; yet later he wrote a letter—known to us as 1 Peter—replete with Old Testament quotations—from the Law, the Prophets, Psalms, and Proverbs. Jesus didn't give the disciples a handout of selected passages to be memorized. He modeled an attitude and devotion that spurred them to imitation. He lived a life that attracted others to Him.

Simply put, most lessons are better "caught than taught." And, not surprisingly, if there is a discrepancy between our talk and our walk, students will be far more likely to do what we do, not what we say. Bryan and Walbek illustrated this truth in an experiment with children.[10] Each child in the study played a game with an adult model. The point of the game was to win money. As part of the experiment, a box requesting donations for the poor was placed in the room where the game was played. Each adult model made mention of the box; some spoke in favor of donating and the value of giving, while others maintained that their winnings should be their own and nobody should ask them to give them to someone else. Regardless of their stated position each group of adults gave from their winnings half the time. The results of the experiment demonstrated quite dramatically that the children's benevolent behavior was affected much more by what the adults *did* than by what they *said*. If, for instance, an adult spoke against donating but gave anyway, the children were more likely to give. If the adult spoke in favor of giving but didn't himself donate anything, the children were more likely to imitate the selfish attitude and actions of the adult. In short, the youngsters behaved predominantly according to what they saw their models *perform*, regardless of their *words*.

As teachers we must take care that the character and example of our lives are consistent with the message that we speak. They should enhance, not detract from, the lessons we seek to communicate. Well-planned words may aid learning—a good walking and breathing example solidifies it. In overwhelming agreement with this premise, educators point to certain factors in modeling that aid in retention of life-changing lessons. Life-changing learning via modeling is best achieved in the presence of:

- *Continuous, frequent, long-term contact with the model.*
- *Development of a genuine caring relationship with the model.*
- *High degrees of exposure to emotional, intellectual, and spiritual characteristics of the model.*
- *Contact with the model in a wide array of life situations, locales, and circumstances.*
- *Utilization of flexibility/spontaneity/mobility in communication and application of the lessons with the model.*
- *Verbal lessons consistent with the modeled behavior.*
- *Consistency in modeled behavior.* [11]

Of course, these characteristics of a good model are notably evident in the teaching style of Jesus. Even a cursory examination of His ministry with the twelve disciples will show how the Teacher utilized modeling. Education experts in ministry today must find ways to take advantage of these known pedagogical principles and discover ways to implement them in their own ministries. Some things simply can't be taught by talk.

It is in this spirit that Abraham J. Heschel observes that "what we need more than anything else is not *textbooks* but text-people. It is the personality of the teacher which is the text that the pupils read; the text they will never forget." [12]

To follow in the footsteps of Jesus the Teacher is a tall order. It means emulating, as men and women, His strategy of incarnation: seeking to identify with those to whom we bring the Gospel message; coming not as experts with all the answers, but as learners seeking to understand the needs of others so that we can meet them; and consistently modeling our message so that our lives and conduct reinforce rather than contradict the Truth we proclaim. The prospect is almost overwhelming. Wouldn't it be easier just to prepare a lesson and deliver it from behind the podium? Can't we retreat to rhetoric and still get the Word out? Not if we seek to follow the Master's model. And time has proven that His way is the best way.

I don't know who said it first, but whoever it was, they were certainly on target: "Many teachers have tried to explain everything—they changed little or nothing. Jesus explained little and changed everything."

Beginning Steps . . .

1. *Make a composite sketch of your students. Who are they? What common quality has drawn them into your class—age? sex? a special interest? List their general characteristics and needs. What effect should such knowledge have on your biblical presentation?*

2. *Mentally walk through "a day in the life" of the people you teach. What makes them tick? What pressures do they face? What do they do to unwind? What are their hopes and dreams? Identify potential lesson topics and activities relevant to their life needs and situations.*

3. *Make an appointment to visit each student in an informal setting—on the job, at school, at home—once during the coming quarter. If your class is large, divide the list of students with another team-teacher, plan outings with two or three students at a time, or spread your visits out over a longer period.*

4. *Summarize the key lessons you want to communicate to your students. Describe the way(s) you can implement them in your own life and list available opportunities, both within and without the classroom, for modeling these lessons.*

When God wanted to communicate to us the
good news of salvation, how did God do it?
God came to us, as love incarnate.
—**Mortimer Arias**

It's an economy of life. You've got a limited amount
of time in which to have an effect. The greatest
way to have impact is by building your life into
other people who are going to outlive you.
This educational philosophy is based
on the Christological model.
—**Howard Hendricks**

Incarnational Educators . . .

- Target their audience,
- Utilize a relationally based style of communication,
- And take seriously the time that is needed to change lives.

CHAPTER FOUR

EDUCATION AS INCARNATION: TARGETING, RELATING, TAKING THE TIME

D r. Richard Selzer, surgeon and author, writes the following:

I stand by the bed where a young woman lies, her face postoperative, her mouth twisted in palsy, clownish. A tiny twig of the facial nerve, the one to the muscles of her mouth, has been severed. She will be thus from now on. The surgeon had followed with religious fervor the curve of her flesh; I promise you that. Nevertheless, to remove the tumor in her cheek, I had to cut the little nerve.

Her young husband is in the room. He stands on the opposite side of the bed, and together, they seem to dwell in the evening lamplight, isolated from me, private. . . .

The young woman speaks. "Will my mouth always be like this?" she asks.

"Yes," I say, "it will. It is because the nerve was cut." She nods and is silent. But the young man smiles.

"I like it," he says. "It's kind of cute."

All at once I know who he is. I understand and I lower my gaze. One is not bold in an encounter with a god. Unmindful, he bends to kiss her crooked mouth, and I so close I can see how he twists his own lips to accommodate hers, to show her that their kiss still works. I remember that the gods appeared in ancient Greece as mortals, and

I hold my breath and let the wonder in.[1]

The words from Selzer's account are penetrating—"bend, twist, accommodate." They vividly describe incarnation, the redemptive adjustment of ourselves to maximize our communication with loved ones, students. Good teachers, like Jesus, are constantly seeking ways to fully adapt themselves to the perspectives of others in order to relay the Good News. When this identification is done well, people find themselves "holding their breath, and letting the wonder in."

Our discussion of incarnation continues with a further investigation of this vital aspect of Jesus' educational strategy.

Target Your Audience

An incarnational teaching model based on Jesus' educational strategy means a limited ministry. You simply cannot be "in the flesh" in a qualitative sense to an unlimited number of people. If you desire to teach effectively, you must identify, learn, and embody truth with a relatively small cluster of individuals. That is part of the genius of Jesus. At a time of apparent success and visibility when it seems natural that He would seek greater exposure, Jesus seems to pull back and focus His efforts on a small group. Why? Tom Sine, in his book *The Mustard Seed Conspiracy,* perhaps says it best: "Jesus let us in on an astonishing secret. God has chosen to change the world . . . through the conspiracy of the insignificant. He chose a ragged bunch of Semite slaves to become the insurgents of His new order. He sent a vast army to flight with three hundred men carrying lamps and blowing horns. He chose an undersized shepherd boy with a slingshot to lead His chosen people. And who would have ever dreamed that God would choose to work through a baby in the cow stall to turn this world right side up! 'God chose the weak things . . . the lowly things . . . the despised things . . . the things that are not . . . so that no one may boast before Him' (1 Cor. 1:27-29, NIV)."[2]

The conspiracy of the insignificant—in many ways that is the crux of the teaching style of Jesus. He limits Himself. He is

born of poor parents in an obscure corner of the earth. He
never travels more than a couple hundred miles from His
home. He never writes a book or runs for office. His resume
is really most unimpressive. His vocational choice ensures
virtual poverty for the duration of His life. And to top it off,
He chooses to surround Himself with commoners whom He
expects to teach and inspire to reach the world with His
message.

At first glance it certainly doesn't strike the observer as
much of a strategy. And yet, notice the brilliance of Jesus'
approach. Knowing that His tenure on earth as a teacher
would be brief, He targeted a geographic area, a particular
group of people, and a point in historical time and space, in
order to relate closely with a handful of teachable men. The
teacher who emulates Jesus at this point will be forced to
make some of the same decisions that God incarnate had to
face. "Where should I focus my efforts?" we will ask. "What
kinds of people do I ultimately want to reach with my ministry and who can I begin training to reach those people?" "Am
I willing to renounce momentary ease, fame, and wealth, if
need be, to fulfill my educational task?" "Where are the few
people out of the larger crowd in whom God would especially
have me invest my life?"

Those of us who honestly desire to be like Jesus the
Teacher must pursue answers to these questions. And the
answers can be painful to accept if our eyes are not fixed
solely on the objective. Our world advocates instant success.
Many of us have grown up enjoying the convenience of instant coffee, minute rice, and heat in seconds via the micro-
wave oven. We want results—and now! To suit our penchant
for efficiency we want not only quick results but big ones,
with a minimum of effort. Far be it from us to devote a
lifetime to people and projects that much of the world deems
insignificant. No, we want our lives to count and our success-
es to be quickly apparent.

Teaching with Christlike methodology takes a different approach. We must determine to target—that is, concentrate
our focus and efforts on a time, place, and audience if we

desire to imitate the Master. Incarnate outreach by one person does not happen quickly, all over the world at once, and with large groups of people—media tools notwithstanding. Jesus Himself did not operate that way, and we can't be expected to. We must choose a few folks in whom to invest our lives and allow them the chance to grow in grace. Our vision must be to equip them to become incarnate, "Jesus style," in the times, in the places, and with the people God chooses for them.

Lest we forget, there is a paradox to this mode of operation—limited though it is initially. Simply put: with time, a vision for the future, trust in the Word of God and reliance on the Holy Spirit it will pay big dividends. Jesus did reach "all the world"—but not in His lifetime. That mission was fulfilled by the men and women He taught and trained and by their spiritual offspring. The patience required by the incarnational approach paid off.

As Christian teachers, we must learn to apply this lesson where we live and work. You can bet that if we don't practice this methodology for the kingdom's sake, someone else will appropriate it for other purposes. For instance, note this brief passage I saw once from *Paix Et Liberte*, a French Communist publication: "The Gospel is a much more powerful weapon for the renewal of society than is our Marxist philosophy. All the same, it is we who will finally beat you. We are only a handful and you Christians are numbered by the millions. But if you remember the story of Gideon and his three hundred companions, you will understand why I am right."

This "Gideon-style" pedagogical philosophy has always been an integral part of the Communist movement. When Karl Marx died in 1883, it appeared as if his theories would die with him. They were, in essence, revolutionary ideas without a revolutionary. But, as we know, his death was not to be the last chapter of the story. Later in the same decade a young Russian named Lenin not only read Engels and Marx, but thoroughly digested their ideology and made it a part of his lifeblood. In a few years he penned *What Is to Be Done*, in which he relayed his desire to translate the theory of Marx and

Engels into action. But how? Lenin asserted that "with a handful of dedicated people who will give me their lives, I will control the world." Was this rash statement an empty boast? He gathered his handful of revolutionaries and today over half the world is Communist, which suggests that his words were neither rash nor empty. He targeted a few and the rest is history. Communists today still employ such methods, as Douglas Hyde points out in *Dedication and Leadership*. Says Hyde, " . . .it is probably true to say of the Communists that never in man's history has a small group of people set out to win a world and achieved more in less time . . . they have always worked through a minority."[3] His book, which describes the movement's effective methodology, is memorable in its premise that a few, imbued with a sense of mission and equipped for service, can shake the world.

The concept works wherever it is found. Several corporations, for instance, have picked up on this formula. I became familiar with one instance a few years back. While researching my doctoral dissertation, I visited Dr. Robert E. Coleman at Trinity Evangelical Divinity School, discussing discipleship techniques and Jesus as a teacher. In our conversation he repeatedly emphasized the effectiveness of the "targeted small group." At one point he looked at me and said, "Matt, some of the best discipling going on today happens outside the confines of the structured church program . . . the concepts [of Jesus' teaching style] work regardless of who utilizes it." Coleman's eyes then darted around his office, checking the bookshelves for a manual put out by an American corporation. He pulled down a notebook entitled *The Master Concepts of Leadership Development*, the management training manual of the particular company. Coleman indicated that in a single year at least two thousand managers had completed the program.

Interestingly enough, that manual was adapted, sometimes word for word, from Coleman's best seller *The Master Plan of Evangelism*. The table of contents is exactly the same, and the concepts are identical to those in Coleman's work. This corporation adapted his book, based on the teaching and evangelistic techniques of Jesus, into a usable training program. I excerpt here a small portion to give you an idea of how it was used.

The welfare and growth of your entire organization should be your highest priority. Obviously, when your organization expands into outlying areas you cannot provide the personal leadership it requires. The growth of the organization will slow down if you are unable to train others to provide the personal leadership you have exhibited.

You began your business some time ago with a small group of people. How many of them were impressive in their outward qualifications? It did not really matter. You were committed to this nucleus of people and you concentrated your efforts on building them into leaders. You selected the people who would make your organization grow and you began to build. . . . What happened was that you developed a strong foundation of leadership. The results were slow in the beginning but by being selective and by concentrating on developing other leaders your organization has grown in strength. Now, with hundreds of people in your organization, you cannot possibly train each one to be as effective as you are. You can, however, develop a select few—look at them as "building blocks" for future foundations.

Concentrating your efforts on a few does not mean neglecting other distributors within your organization. The farsighted approach is to "rifle" your efforts into building a strong foundation.

Says Coleman, "There's not a word in there that would give you any indication that this is religious. Nothing is said about God or about Christ; nothing is said about faith, or grace, or redemption, or forgiveness . . . but do you see a similarity between that and *The Master Plan of Evangelism?*"

I discovered, during my time with him, another twist to the story. The corporation in question did not request Dr. Coleman's permission to use the material, or even give him credit. One of Coleman's friends asked indignantly if he was going to sue. He chuckled, recounting the memory. "Why, no," he replied, "at least with some businessmen, I must have gotten the message across. I haven't been nearly as effective with most church leaders I know!" But he added quickly, "I believe the world could be evangelized in this generation if we really took these ideas to heart and practiced them. All we have to do," relates this professor, "is follow the example of Jesus."

The lesson hasn't been entirely lost on religious activists. Dean Kelly, in *Why Conservative Churches Are Growing,* notes that the great mobilizers are frequently religious leaders who draw to themselves little groups of followers. These bands are characterized by, among other things, a commitment to one another in mutually supportive, like-minded fellowship. Kelly writes: "These little bands of committed men and women have an impact on history out of all proportion to their numbers or apparent difficulties. In the main, they are usually recruited from the least promising ranks of society: they are not noble or wealthy or well educated or particularly talented. . . ."[4]

But, says Kelly, these gathered individuals "are able to cut through the partial and fleeting commitments of the rest of society like a buzz saw through peanut brittle." Why? Because these zealots take their cue from the "great mobilizers" who know that targeted small groups, linked together and willing to subordinate their personal desires and ambitions to a great cause, are "intensely and continuously so much more alive" than other enthusiasts in lesser causes.

The greatest of mobilizers, Jesus the Teacher, recognized the targeting of time and effort on a small group as a vital aspect of incarnation. Whether applied in political organizations, industry, or Christian endeavor, Jesus' example on this principle underscores a truth that works.

Relationships

In the third chapter of Genesis God asks man and woman a question that must have been rather disconcerting. Adam and Eve have sinned for the first time and are on the run in the Garden of Eden. Hiding behind some trees, they hear the voice of God ask, "Where are you?" The question wasn't for God's benefit—He already knew. But He wanted His people to recognize their true position. Exactly a chapter later, five words posed to the next generation are equally as penetrating: "Where is Abel your brother?" These are penetrating questions apropros to all believers. Where are we in relationship to our God? And where is that person to whom you were meant to relate as brother or as sister? Are you loving them and building bridges to them, or hurting them and putting distance between yourselves? The answers should have a dramatic impact on our approach to teaching.

God wants to know where we are, first of all, in loving, trusting, and honoring relationship to Him. There is nothing more basic to Christian education. This is easy to see, for instance, in the prayer life of the Master. It is quite obvious from the Gospel accounts that Jesus continually sought the face of God and enjoyed constant contact with the Father. This is an imperative pattern for all who truly desire to emulate the incarnational model of Jesus. At every crucial point of His life and at all times in between, Jesus stole away in search of a lonely place to be with the Father. The fact is, prayer was so much a part of Jesus' life that a prayerless Christlike educator is a contradiction in terms.

In the godly Jewish home in which Jesus grew up He would have been well-grounded in the habit of prayer. Two disciplines were required of the pious Jew of that day: he was exhorted to recite the *Shema* (Deut. 6:4-9) twice a day and to observe the three hours of prayer, in the morning, at three in the afternoon and in the evening around sundown. At each of the three hours, a Jew would faithfully recite the *Tephilla*, "the prayer of prayers" which included a litany of blessings. In the morning and evening the *Shema* would precede the *Tephilla* and personal petitions would close each of the three hours of prayer.[5]

The fact that He had set times for prayer obviously did not deter Jesus from praying at other times as well. The Gospel of Luke, known as the "Gospel of Prayer," paints an interesting picture of Jesus in contact with the Father. Prayer was an essential part of His life in times of crisis or transition. For instance, Luke records that Jesus prayed:

- at His baptism (3:21)
- before the choosing of His twelve disciples (6:12)
- before His question of the disciples: "Who do you say that I am?" (9:18ff)
- at the Transfiguration (9:28ff)
- upon the cross (23:46)

Further, Luke notes perhaps the greatest lesson about Jesus and prayer. As Jesus' popularity rose and people demanded more and more of His time and physical resources, Scripture records that He "often withdrew to lonely places and prayed" (Luke 5:16, NIV). Jesus taught about prayer, engaged in a regular pattern of liturgy and intercession, prayed at the pivotal points in His career, and frequently slipped away from busyness to stay in communion with His Father.

Captain Eugene McDaniel, a Navy pilot shot down in Vietnam, became a prisoner held captive for six years. He speaks to the vital need for communication in a life. POWs, he relates, die much sooner if they don't communicate. Time and again, McDaniel and others would risk death and torture to work out and execute a complicated communications system. They would write under plants, cough, sing, tap on walls, laugh, flap laundry, and use numerous other techniques to transmit a letter of the alphabet. Says the Captain, "The lone, isolated being becomes weak, vulnerable. I knew I had to make contact, no matter what the cost."[6] Life, whether you are in a Vietnam prison cell or in an American Sunday School class, depends on it! For Christian educators, communication with the Almighty is essential for strength and vitality in our endeavor. Jesus knew this and pursued it. So must we.

"Where are you?" the Educator asks us today. Are we as teachers seeking to emulate the Master, spending time cultivating our spiritual lives as Jesus did His? If God incarnate felt the need to nurture a divine relationship, how much more should we?

Educator: do you have a daily, established program of prayer and Bible study? Do you consider such communication from and with God one of the most important duties that you perform as teacher or parent? When the pressing needs of your educational tasks clamor for attention, do you—as did Jesus—often slip away to a quiet place to pray? Affirmative answers to these questions denote positive first steps enroute to the most important of all relationships for Christian communicators.

The writer of Hebrews exhorts us to be "fixing our eyes upon Jesus, the author and perfecter of faith" (12:2). The most important calling of Christian educators is to be intimately and daily acquainted with the One whose love we desire to communicate. Such a relationship is not an elective; it is a required resource for the teacher of truth. We must seek God rather than hiding midst the "trees of the garden" (Gen. 3:8) that inhibit closer communion with Him. We will find it impossible to convincingly recommend to others someone whom we ourselves do not know well.

The divine-human relationship, though primary, is not the only relationship imperative to our educational task. God created us social beings, so other relationships quickly follow. When Jesus was challenged by a lawyer to articulate the most important commandment, He quoted two Scriptures out of the Torah (see Matt. 22:35ff). The first was, "You shall love the Lord your God with all your heart and with all your soul and will all your might (Deut. 6:5). If you want to know the answer to God's question, "Where are you in relationship to Me?" measure yourself by that passage. Then, without hesitating, Jesus cited another verse: "You shall love your neighbor as yourself" (Lev. 19:18). The second commandment pinpoints how well we are doing in relationship to our brothers and sisters. Christian educators must take the second major question of God in Genesis very seriously. There is great truth contained in the following formula:

Communication = Content + Relationship[7]

Educational communication, of course, infers certain content which needs to be transmitted. At best, though, content is but half of the sum. To become too content-oriented inhibits real growth. Relationships should be a chief consideration. Even the word communication lends itself to this position. The word commune comes from the Latin word *communis* meaning "common." Similarly, communicate comes from *communi*, meaning "care." To truly communicate we must dare to establish some common ground and loving care. As these elements increase, so will the potential for effective communication.

Klaus Wegenast posits an interesting etymology for the Greek word for teach.[8] He claims that the word *didasko* comes from the root *dek-* meaning "to accept" or "extend the hand to." The other parts of the word convey the idea of repeated action, i.e., repeatedly offering the hand for acceptance—a clear call to relationship. The art of teaching at its best is just that. We establish a close personal relationship and through that conduit open up the possibilities for learning.

Some people seem to have an innate gift for achieving rapport with those with whom they desire to communicate. I have always wondered what the key to this is. One of my students handed me a book recently that included some of the underlying reasons for successful communication capabilities. The necessary ingredients are illustrated by the following graph.[9]

Steps toward effective interpersonal relationships.

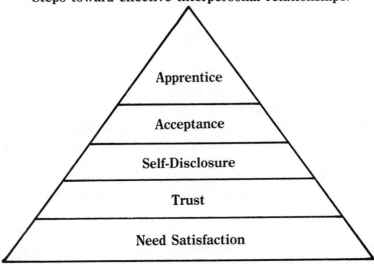

Let's take a look at these various steps toward effective interpersonal relationships:

Need Satisfaction: Many individual needs are met through the dynamic of interpersonal relationships. Good communicators make efforts to come to grips with the needs of the other participant(s) in the interpersonal process and try to meet those concerns. Frequently, verbal interaction alone satisfies. Over a longer period of time, needs can be met in other, more tangible ways that have more substantial and longlasting effects. One of the pillars of incarnational impact is "find the need, and meet it."

Trust: The incarnational communicator moves quickly to develop trust. If needs are met appropriately and with sensitivity then the trust level necessary for a good relationship is easy to attain. "Will this person continue to help me?" is one of the questions that participants need to answer affirmatively if trust is to be developed. Over the long-term, consistent benevolent behavior is a must for development of trust.

Self-disclosure: This is the process of making yourself known to the ones with whom you are seeking to interrelate and allowing them to make themselves known to you. Again, this is accomplished as trust is developed, but care needs to be exercised here. As one of my professors once said, "Don't hit a thumbtack with a sledgehammer!" To reveal too much too soon results in overdisclosure, which may be threatening and can hamper communication as much as—sometimes more than—superficiality or underdisclosure.

Acceptance: When people disclose themselves to you, then you must accept them. Rejection reproduces itself, so does acceptance. The incarnate teacher wants to lead people to greater things, always with the attitude that "I love you and am committed to you" regardless. One of the Hebrew wordbooks I have seen translates lovingkindness (*hesed*) as "obstinate love"—loving them through thick and thin. That is acceptance!

Apprentice: Here is the peak. Once the first four steps are accomplished, the interpersonal educator can begin to expect opportunities for some serious teaching and learning. But notice the word apprentice. It does not denote education from afar. The word apprentice comes from the Latin *ad-* meaning "to" and *prehendere-* which means "to seize." Having "seized" attention, you will maintain it through close relationship. This is teaching and learning not by lecture, but by education "in the flesh" through an intimate interpersonal dynamic.

Good communicators/teachers are able to progress through these levels and arrive at an apprentice relationship with the learner, whether it happens in a matter of minutes or a matter of years. Some teachers, blessed with effervescent personalities, achieve this almost by second nature. Most of us, however, have to work hard at the process. The job of educators, trying to be like the incarnate Jesus, is to understand these stages of relational development and take the steps and correctives necessary to become more effective communicators of our love and His.

Discovering how to work toward the achievement of satisfying relationships is no small part of teaching. In fact, researchers have noted how very important such an endeavor can be to our Christian task. For instance, the Institute of American Church Growth recognizes that people who become involved in the local church do so primarily through relationships. Of those who *come through the church doors:*

- 79 percent do so through relationships with friends;
- 6 percent through a pastor;
- 5 percent through Sunday School;
- 3 percent walk in uninvited;
- 3 percent are attracted by the program;
- 2 percent because of a special need;
- 1 percent as a result of visitation; and
- .5 percent after an evangelistic crusade. [10]

Such statistics show that one of the most vital educational strategies is building bridges to people through our "webs of common kinship, common community, and common interests." Relationships are the most powerful means we have to fully communicate the good news of Christ. No matter how clever and effective our techniques and teaching might be, nothing beats the powerful effect of intimate relationships riding tan-

THE MASTER PLAN OF TEACHING

dem with redemptive purpose for making disciples. To realize this is to understand what Jesus was trying to do by relating intimately with a handful of good-hearted followers. It is a strategy of explosive potential.

Incarnation: It Takes Time

Incarnational ministry works. Through identification, assuming the posture of a learner, embodying the message, appropriately targeting an audience, and developing healthy and intimate relationships, the educator has a far greater chance of effecting lasting life change.

However, it takes time. One of the primary lessons of the incarnate Jesus is that one had better be prepared for a marathon rather than a sprint. He took thirty-three years to accomplish His specific objective in Palestine. He clocked in countless hours with His disciples—sticking with them through their best and through their worst. Sometimes it must have been discouraging. They often seemed to miss the whole point of what He was saying. But Jesus persevered. He patiently explained, loved them even in their failures, and continued to live, speak, and do the Truth before them. The disciples didn't even grasp the full significance of Jesus' mission until after the Resurrection.

Eventually His message began to take hold. And blossom. We read in Acts 3 and 4 of a transformed Peter and John. Peter was no longer the fisherman who fearfully denied Jesus, nor John the Son of Thunder who argued for his own greatness. No, these men boldly healed and proclaimed. And when arrested and called before the Sanhedrin, they didn't flinch. The rulers, elders, and scribes were certainly surprised. "Now as they observed the confidence of Peter and John, and understood that they were uneducated and untrained men, they were marveling, and began to recognize them as having been with Jesus" (Acts 4:13). The secret to their transformation was not simply that they had been among the crowds who heard Jesus' powerful teaching. Many followed to that extent, but we don't see them fearlessly confronting the Jewish powers-that-be. These men had *been with Jesus*. They had walked, talked, and traveled with Him for nearly three years. And even though it took a while, the Truth and power of His Person had finally penetrated their hearts. That wouldn't have happened except that Jesus stuck with the men He chose and poured His life into theirs, day in and day out.

In the same way, contemporary teachers can expect to spend a good bit of concentrated time in one place to accomplish ministry goals. Examples abound of everyday folk who take seriously this vital educational aspect. I go no farther than my own local church for one of my favorite examples. The Rev. Keith Tonkel has been at our little inner-city church in Jackson, Mississippi for twenty-one years now. When his family arrived, there was only a handful of members left in the church from a once robust congregation. The building was located in one of Jackson's "changing communities." Those economically able to move out were doing so, leaving the rest behind. The Tonkels made the sacrifice of time, money, and personal prestige, however, and now, over twenty years later, the church bustles with activity. It is packed on Sunday mornings and laity-led ministries have spread all over the inner city of Jackson and beyond from the humble springboard of Wells Church on Bailey Avenue.

But again, it took time and sacrifice. Tonkel, a vivacious personality and delightful speaker, has had to turn down many prestigious positions to stay put. As a result, his church is an exciting place of ministry because he has adopted the attitude that success is not necessarily more exposure, money, prestige, or power. Says Tonkel, "I really believe that Christ calls us into a lot of situations that don't measure success in the world's terms. I think that success is measured in terms of faithfulness to incarnational ministry. If we make room in our society for those who always want to climb the ladder to the better position, shouldn't we also make room for those who find it important to not keep moving away from one church to take the better appointment?"

At Wells, lives are being changed; the Gospel is taught through activated love, and the community is being served. It is the result of a pastoral family deciding to set down their roots in a place that most people try to avoid. But yet it is more, as Keith describes: "This is not the story of a preacher who stayed. Wells is the story of a people. You are going to write about how great it is to stay in a place and pay the price. But there are several folks in this church who have turned down moves and promotions and evangelistic pleas to come to bigger and prettier churches here in town to stay here and serve. Remember, incarnational ministry has to result in a people who decide to be incarnational as well. That is the story here."

The testimonies of churches across the land are beginning to show that agents of change frequently will be those who stay in their places of ministry six to ten years or more. Examination of solid, growing churches everywhere is pointing out that that is the price of redemptive change in people's lives. Says Tonkel: "You have to stay a while before people believe it when you say you love them. You have to be incarnate a while before they begin to sense your dreams and share them with you. It takes time for people to see you as a fellow struggler rather than simply the appointed pastor sent by the bishop."

Not long ago, one of our friends came over to our recently purchased house and mentioned that since we decided to stay in the community she felt much more apt to pursue an intimate relationship with us. "Now that I know you all aren't going to pick up and leave any time soon, I think I'll begin to trust you a bit more!" Having studied educational incarnation, I think I knew what she meant.

Re-incarnation

Some morning, when you really need to wake up the sleepy-eyed participants in your Sunday School class, Bible study, or worship service, try the following: Mention that, after carefully examining the evidence, you now wholeheartedly affirm the Christian doctrine of "re-incarnation." I have tried this a time or two, and for startling a crowd there are few things better. For the benefit of your own health and safety you'll find it best to quickly explain exactly what you mean. The prefix "re-"

means simply "to do again." Re-incarnation redefined means to "pitch a tent" in the midst of the people you desire to teach, following the example of Jesus the Teacher. It can happen as we allow the Spirit of Christ to dwell in us and transform us. As we do that, our teaching will be revolutionized.

As Christian educators — in the pulpit or the Sunday School class, in the home or in the workplace — have we allowed the Educator in us to reign so that the testimony of our lives serves to remind the world of Him? Has the message of good news and incarnation taken on flesh and bone in the lives of His disciples? We should affirm the doctrine of re-incarnation and strive to be holy educators as He is the holy Educator — the Word lived through our flesh. If we allow the Lord and His Word to do that in our lives, what a difference we will make for the kingdom of God.

Beginning Steps...

1. *Interview someone who is successful at small group discipleship, or review a book on the subject, for pointers on targeting potential small-group members. Identify five prospects and begin praying for them and your potential input into their lives. After several weeks of praying, ask the Lord when and how you might challenge them to paticipate in a small group with you.*

2. *Schedule a regular quiet time for prayer and Bible study. From the following list, select one or two items that appeal to you and incorporate them into your time as well.*
   — Scripture memorization — Write verses to be learned on 3"x5" cards or purchase pre-printed cards.
   — Hymnbook — Singing or reading great hymns of the church can revitalize the devotional life.
   — Journal — Keep a notebook to jot down insights in your spiritual pilgrimage.
   — Fasting — Consider devoting one or more meal time(s) per week to praying rather than eating.
   — Devotional classics — There are certain books which have been read and loved by generations of Christians. Your pastor

or local Christian bookstore can recommend a few. Try reading a portion each day.

—Biographies—The life stories of faithful men and women can inspire and challenge.

3. Using Grunlan and Mayer's relational diagram on page 63, chart individual students at the level of your relationship with them. Are there any steps you can take to facilitate an elevated level of interpersonal interaction? List the possibilities.

*The great end of life is not knowledge, but action.
What men need is as much knowledge as they can
organize for action; give them more and
it may become injurious. Some men
are heavy and stupid from
undigested learning.*

—Thomas Huxley

*My mother and my brothers are these who
hear the Word of God and do it.*

—Jesus

To Educate Like Jesus, the Teacher Must . . .

- Teach *with* activity, *for* activity,
- Develop a TBWA (teaching by walking around) model that utilizes a situational emphasis,
- Remember that we were created *for good works*,
- Provide our students with *relevant* movement.

CHAPTER FIVE

ACTIVATING CHARACTER: HOLINESS ON THE MOVE

S uppose it was that geese could talk," begins the 19th century philosopher Soren Kierkegaard in a journal entry entitled "The Tame Geese." With that imaginative beginning, the Danish existentialist proceeds to paint a verbal picture of a land in which geese could not only speak but were also in the habit of waddling to church every Sunday. The presiding gander would honk eloquent sermons about the high goal of their Creator and such motivational topics as God's generous gift to these fowl—wings. With the aid of these feathery propellers, the geese were told, they could "fly away to distant regions, blessed climes, where properly they were at home, for here they were only strangers." It was indeed exciting for the geese to gather on Sunday mornings; at their sacred meetings they would, in their ecstacy, curtsy and bow and undoubtedly send feathers flying about the sanctuary.

"And so it was every Sunday" writes Kierkegaard. But a strange phenomenon repeated itself weekly, for after the geese had enjoyed the fellowship of their congregation, worshipped the great Goose God in the sky, and heard an outstanding message, they would adjourn and, muses Kierkegaard, "Each would waddle home to his own affairs."

Did you get that? After hearing of a generous Creator, wings, the possibility of flight, and the blessed climes and regions which awaited them—with a short honk or two thrown in to resemble some "Amens!"—the geese all *waddled home!* And to the delight of hungry human mouths everywhere they "throve and were well liked, became plump and delicate—and then were eaten . . . and that was the end of it."[1]

This sobering story by the "Disturbing Dane" is one of the many parables Kierkegaard wrote poking fun at the Christians in Copenhagen. These were folks who he felt were willing to listen to messages and attend services, yet were unwilling to set sail with the wings of faith and imagination God had granted them. Contained in this brief story is the premier challenge to Christian education in every age. Intellectual, emotional, and even pseudo-spiritual assent simply is not the goal. God wants a life of movement for the Kingdom. He wants us to fly for Him.

Those of us in Christian education soon discover that not only is doing—or flying or running or walking—a matter of obedience, it also makes for good learning. Confucius, for instance, asserted that, "I hear, and I forget. I see and I remember. I do, and I understand." Modern educators, in the same vein, will frequently cite the following numbers as indicative of the educational process:

We remember . . .
10% of what we **hear**
50% of what we **say**
70% of what we **see**
90% of what we **do**

There is a bit of irony in our consideration of these statistics. Most educators know that activity is the best way to learn. Hearing a message is but a small part of the kind of learning which results in positive life change. But educational programs are not normally structured for an effective blend of hearing, saying, seeing, and doing. We are much more inclined to offer our pupils the chance to hear only. Thus, we see little result. Tests have shown the inefficiency of simply listening to a message. For instance, after listening to a ten-minute presentation, the average listener has heard and comprehended about half of what was said. Within forty-eight hours, however, that drops another 50 percent to a 25 percent effectiveness level. By the end of the week the listeners will be down to 10 percent or less![2] Forcing people to sit quietly and listen is setting them up for incredibly poor retention. Says Howard Hendricks, "Unfortunately, the bulk of Christian education is hearing oriented. That's why it's often so inefficient."[3]

Jesus knew that all four elements were necessary for instruction to have lasting impact. The crowning jewel of His methodology was His penchant for "learning by doing." The effectiveness of Jesus' approach lay in taking His message from the lofty ivory tower confines of the theoretical and theological to the cutting edge of living. For instance, in the Book of Matthew—known as the "teaching Gospel"—Jesus very clearly sets out the great outline of His kingdom in five major discourses. But of no less significance is the fact that interwoven throughout the book is the story of "Jesus—Man of Action." He heals, cleanses lepers, stills the sea, forgives, fellowships with sinners, instructs the apostles and sends them out to service, debates with the scribes and Pharisees, feeds the masses, prays, challenges individuals evangelistically, cleanses the temple; and eventually endures betrayal, suffering, and death before rising from the dead and commissioning His disciples to a worldwide task. Today, we remember the parables, preaching, and teachings of Jesus—and for good reason. They were words with wings. They proved their power in the day-to-day living of the one who spoke them. He was a teacher on the move.

Jesus wanted His disciples to have maximum righteous effect upon their world. If what has been said thus far about the impact of *doing* upon learning is true, it is only natural that Jesus taught not only *with* activity but *for* activity as well. Action was a crucial element of His educational approach. He was holiness on the move.

Teaching with Activity

Kierkegaard once noted that "There are many people who reach their conclusions about life like schoolboys: they cheat their master by copying the answer out of a book without having worked the sum out for themselves."[4] The ultimate result is that, though they may be able to pass some kind of classroom or written test, those who take this shortcut have done themselves a terrible disservice. They neither intellectually grasp the material nor internalize its message. Jesus would have nothing to do with such a halfhearted effort at learning. His disciples were required to test their new-found Good News on the cutting edge of life.

My wife has studied Hebrew at the seminary where I teach. I used to quiz her occasionally to see what interesting insights she might have gained in her studies for the class. She informed me one day that the Hebrew word commonly translated "know" (*yada*) more accurately means "to experience." The thought fascinated me so I strolled over to the language professor's office and asked him firsthand about the word. Glancing up from his work, he reiterated what Mary had already told me. "It means 'to experience' or 'to encounter,' " he explained.

"That's great!" I beamed, clapping my hands together. "It'll make for a terrific illustration in my book, right?"

"Matt," my friend corrected me, "it's not an illustration, it's the point."

"The point?" I replied quizzically. He went on to explain.

The Hebrew word is used in a variety of ways in the Old Testament. For instance, he suggested turning to the discussion of Cain's conception in Genesis 4:1. As the Scripture puts it, "Adam *knew* Eve his wife" (RSV). In other words, he experienced or encountered Eve sexually. From there the word appears in many contexts throughout the Old Testament narrative, but at its most profound level it expressed the desire of God that His people would *know* Him—not just intellectually, but in a much more intimate and experiential sense. They would experience their God—love Him, interact with Him, develop an intimacy with Him, and act on His behalf. Marvin

Wilson, in his discussion of *yada* notes that:

> *The idea of knowledge thus embraced the whole human personality. A grasp of so much information was not enough; it also implied a response in the practical domain of life, in behavior and morals. . . . In short, for the Hebrew, to "know" was to "do". . . . [It] went far beyond mere intellectual activity; it was to act. It included down-to-earth activity or personal know-how applied to various realms and experiences of life.*[5]

Remember those words, teachers. Knowledge is "response . . . practical . . . behavior . . . morals . . . doing . . . action . . . application." Taking knowledge seriously is more than blackboards, books, memorization, and learning games. It is, in the best and deepest sense, head/heart/hands on the move.

Jesus carried this wholistic concept into the training of His disciples. "Knowing"—experiencing, encountering—was the crux of His method. At first glance, it appears that at the outset of Jesus' learning program such activity was limited. As all rabbinic disciples, the Twelve first of all served Jesus through care for daily matters and menial tasks. They attended to meals, lodging, crowd control, and even some baptisms. However, even as they performed such tasks Jesus was teaching them through His own example of loving and serving. It is worthy of note that as the disciples primarily observed and listened, they were also on the move—working, serving. Could it be that one of the things communicated through the rabbinic model of teaching is that a disciple absorbs and internalizes messages better in the context of activity than by passive listening?

While the tasks that disciples performed under the tutelage of their rabbi were initially less impressive than one might expect for future world-class movers and shakers, the day came when Jesus sent the inner circle of disciples out on a journey of ministry in order that they might preach, cast out demons, and anoint and heal the sick (Mark 6:7ff). It is critical, however, that this mission activity occurred *after* they had seen the Master in action firsthand and had worked closely alongside Him. How they were sent out is notable as well. The Gospel according to Matthew (Matt. 10:1ff) reports four crucial dynamics involved: (1) The disciples were given explicit instructions. They were told what kind of people to concentrate on, specific activities to participate in, how to handle their finances, whom to approach upon arrival in a town, what to do when rejected, what to expect when among "wolves," speaking tips when they found themselves before the officials, and how to deal with their persecutors. (2) They were given verbal encouragement as well as striking challenges. They were told how difficult and potentially dangerous their mission was, but also how much confidence they should have in the proclamation of their message. (3) Each disciple was linked with a companion with whom to work as a team in their journeys. This "buddy system" provided sharpening, encouragement, and increased overall effectiveness in what would prove to be a demanding season of ministry. (4) Though physically separated from Him, they were ministering alongside their rabbi; He was involved in parallel activity elsewhere. "It came about that when Jesus finished giving instructions to His twelve disciples, He departed from there to teach and preach in their cities" (Matt. 11:1).

Jesus later presented a similar ministry challenge to a wider circle of disciples, "the seventy." These followers, although not a part of the group who constantly accompanied Jesus, were nonetheless expected to move out into their world and work for the Kingdom. They received nearly the same instructions as the Twelve (Luke 10:1ff) and were said to have "returned with joy." Jesus delighted in their reports and exclaimed with a note of ecstacy, "I was watching Satan fall from heaven like lightning. Behold, I have given you authority to tread upon serpents and scorpions, and over all the power of the enemy, and nothing shall injure you" (Luke 10:18-19).

After uttering these words, Jesus adds this note: "I praise Thee, O Father, Lord of heaven and earth, that Thou didst hide these things from the wise and intelligent and didst reveal them to babes. Yes, Father, for thus it was well-pleasing in Thy sight" (Luke 10:21). Then, turning to the disciples, He remarked privately, "Blessed are the eyes which see the things you see, for I say to you, that many prophets and kings wished to see the things which you see . . . to hear the things you hear" (Luke 10:23-24). Obviously pleased and in a moment of excitement Jesus reiterates what we have asserted. Learning is a direct result of doing. This is as true today as it was 2,000 years ago. It is a fundamental pillar of education.

After the disciples' return from service, Jesus seems to accelerate His "peripatetic (teaching by walking around) model" of education. It was learning *en route*—not as paper and pencil, but through the application of lessons in the real world. Throughout His ministry, Jesus used all kinds of situations and activities to help the disciples learn.

In his book *The Teaching Techniques of Jesus,* Herman Horne poses several piercing questions concerning situational learning and its educational importance:

▲ Can you imagine Jesus letting an [educational] situation slip?

▲ Is it custom for us to use the situation or let it slip? Why?

▲ Shall we conclude that the only kind of teaching Jesus did was situational in character?

▲ If so, we must not neglect to add that He Himself, being what He was, had much to do with causing these occasions to arise.

▲ Also, that He specifically made certain [other] situations. . . .

▲ Which is the greater opportunity for the teacher, the lesson in manners and morals, or some good or bad act in school?

▲ Do you agree that Jesus "certainly was a master opportunist in seizing on every occasion, as it arose, to impact His precepts, and was in vital rapport with both the individuals and the groups He met"?

▲ What difference would it make if we began now to be teachers of the situational rather than the formal type?[6]

If the example of Jesus is our educational ideal, it might force us in our teaching to shift from a primarily traditional classroom focus to an "occasional" or "situational" focus. One of my friends in educational studies contends that if you could read the biographies of the great minds in intellectual history you would not find anyone whose way of thinking was dramatically changed in the classroom. He argues that it was during the informal times of discussion, interaction, dialogue, and service that life-changing insights occurred. In like manner, with the early believers it was Jesus walking along, asking, "But who do you say I am?" (Matt. 16:15); or reclining at a meal, seizing the situation to say, "Simon, I have something to say to you" (Luke 7:40). Powerful teaching? Teaching *en route*, midst everyday events and surroundings possesses great potential impact. Consider the following four approaches to creative teaching:

Case Study #1: One former law professor at Southern Methodist University was a bit unorthodox in his educational approach. His specialty was trial law. He'd set up his classroom like a courtroom, complete with the prosecution, defense, and jury. The mock court would then begin trying the case. It wouldn't be long before the professor—who was supposed to be an innocent bystander—would leap onto the courtroom floor and yell at the prosecution, "Yikes! You're not going to try that case that way, are you?!" The defense would begin feeling smug until the teacher would whip around and say with squinted eyes and furrowed brow, "You know what I'd do with that defense?" before proceeding to shred it to pieces. In the end, the only comfortable folks in the classroom were the judge and jury, and they knew what was coming next week when they would play the other parts. The professor would then smile and say, "Hey, you guys, you want to know how to win this case? Follow me!"

One seminary professor sent his students over to see this man in action. "How will we find him on campus?" they asked. The professor answered, "Just look for a guy on the law campus, and if he's got fifteen guys following him, that's the man!" Says one observer, "This guy has produced more winners in the state of Texas than any five professors put together. I asked one of my lawyer friends what it was like to be in his classes and he said, 'Once you've had that professor, everything in real life is downhill!' "

Said the law professor, "I have just one principle as a teacher. I'd rather have my students lose in here and win out there, than win in here and lose out there."[7]

Case Study #2: Fred Tipton was driving along I-70 through Kansas with his wife and four-year-old son Timmy. Suddenly, along the side of the interstate appeared a family similar to the Tiptons: father, mother, and two small daughters. Fred slowed to a stop, ambled out of his car and helped the stranded family with their car trouble. Back in the car, little Timmy was all questions. "What was wrong, Daddy?" "Was the engine broken?" "Did they have any toys?" Fred patiently answered all the inquiries, but the last question intrigued him most. "What was that man's name, Daddy?"

Fred didn't even blink before replying, "That man's name was Jesus." Timmy, jumping up on the back seat, said, "What?!" "Yes," responded Fred, "the Bible says that when somebody needs help and we are able to help them, it's like we are helping Jesus." Enter the teachable moment, Matthew 25:31-46, Jesus' story of the Good Samaritan.

Is it any wonder that with continuous teaching like that over a period of years the most excited, activated layman in First Church is Dr. Timothy (Timmy) Tipton?

Case Study #3: Julie Gorman, of Fuller Seminary, says our classroom teaching contains a lot of information but precious little formation. She has sought to rectify that imbalance in her own educational efforts. "I want to share myself in a wholistic way. I will do all kinds of things, from taking students with me when I minister to taking them with me when I go shopping. I have them over to do gardening with me or to fix something around the house. Sometimes they will just come over and kick back and we relax together. I've taken them camping and rafting with me as well as to sports events and musicals. Sometimes I will go with them to things, because I don't want them to feel that they just have to come to my turf. In these ways you'll usually have more significant discipling opportunities than you do in the classroom situation. It's real then . . . relevant."

She's not an ordinary professor, perhaps, but certainly one who changes lives.

Case Study #4: Dave Stevens is fond of creating situations in which his church youth group learns together in the midst of adventure. "You tend to learn a thing or two when rappelling down a mountain. When your life depends upon a friend doing his job right, you learn community. You learn patience. You learn trust. You learn discipleship," he says. Or, he enjoys getting a bunch of inner-city kids together to go on a lengthy bike tour. "About the second day, after you've sat down on an unfamiliar seat pedaling unfamiliar strokes, you learn something about pain, and how to cooperate, love, work, and learn regardless of how you feel. You can't discount that kind of discipleship," Stevens comments.

Whether utilized by these teachers or by Jesus Himself, situations and activity are a memorable means of communication. The memories run deep, the lessons are not easily forgotten, and a learning picture endures after eloquent explanations grow blurry. Charles Simeon once wrote that we must learn to screw the truth into the minds of our hearers: "A screw is the strongest of all mechanical powers . . . when it has been turned a few times, scarcely any power can pull it out."[8] I submit that learning through activity is the screw; the teacher, guided by the Christlike Spirit, is the screwdriver who guides the action so as to indelibly imprint a truth into the student. Used appropriately and effectively, activity serves as a valuable tool for memorable learning.

But if the first section in this chapter deals with the use of activity for learning, then the second section must naturally address the use of activity for the end of Christlike service. Activity must be both a means and an end.

Redemptive Activity: The Goal of Jesus

"As a general rule," remarked the great Benjamin Disraeli, "the most successful man in life is the man who has the best information."[9] Appreciating that quote, I would nonetheless add a small corrective. The most successful in life are not merely those who have the best information, but those who act upon that knowledge. Socrates once described an educated man as one who "rarely missed the expedient course of action." What Socrates vocalized was evident in the life and actions of Jesus.

In his 100-page report entitled "1984—Religion in America," George Gallup, Jr., noted the paradox that "Religion is growing in importance among Americans, but morality is losing ground." What makes for this seeming contradiction is the "very little difference" found between "the behavior of the churched and unchurched on a wide range of items including lying, cheating, and pilferage." There is an exception, a remnant so to speak. Twelve percent of the population could be counted among the "highly spiritually committed." They are what Gallup calls "a breed apart." But for the most part, the Christian world too frequently nods "yes" but acts "no."

Unfortunately, we seem to have become a country that emphasizes religious decision instead of religious life change. The difference, of course, can be as wide as the world. To affirm Christianity as a correct belief system does not necessarily include acknowledging the faith as a "by-life" system—that is, by our lives we are Christians, not just by our thoughts. A call to Christ definitely involves a decision, but it is a lifelong commitment to devote the totality of one's life and resources to Him.

A former professor once remarked that "you do what you believe, and you believe what you do." As the years pass I find those words increasingly profound. Once in a job interview I was asked whether or not I considered abortion an affront to Christlike living. Did I believe, for instance, that the "fetus was a human being from the time of conception?" My questioners assumed I would affirm the "pro-life" position and we would proceed to the next item. Instead of reciting the obvious evangelical position, I said, "Frankly, I'm not sure." I was asked to explain.

"Well, if I really believed that the fetus was a human being," I said, "I mean *really, really* believed it, then I would *do* something about the hundreds of abortions performed per month in this city."

I could affirm the intellectual position, but the issue was much deeper. Thinking about our positions and actively allowing our ideas to monitor our living are two entirely different things. Did I really believe it—enough to take action? Like many, the answer was "not really." If we did, would we sit around and merely cast "pro-life" votes instead of participating in appropriate pro-life action, whatever we might individually perceive that to be? The thunder of my inaction drowned out the reply I would like to have made.

In his book *Dedication and Leadership* Douglas Hyde discusses this bond between belief and action:

> *Any Communist tutor who is worth his salt finished each class with these words: "What are the comrades going to do about what they have learned today? How are you going to apply it to the hospital where you are nursing? You in the school where you teach? You in the factory where you are employed? You as a housewife to the neighborhood where you are living?"*
>
> *The first item on the agenda when the class next meets will be: "How did the comrades apply what they learned last week?" It does not matter whether the subject is trade union*

history, scientific socialism, or dialectical materialism, teacher and taught must try to relate it to life and action.
In passing, I would reiterate that this is not the way in which Christianity, for example, is normally taught. .... [10]

Jesus used learning by doing to prepare His disciples for lives of action. His training program was not designed to create "ivory-tower" academicians. He intended to develop disciples who could not only think and feel aright, but because of their thinking and depth of affection be motivated to redemptive action. That is why Jesus' speaking was fortified by doing. That is why He moved among those with the greatest needs. That is why His was a "teaching by walking around" method. Immobility contradicted the very Gospel that He promoted.

Many educators now accept a definition of learning appropriate to discipleship training. Learning, they say, is "a relatively permanent change in behavior that comes as a result of experience or practice." I think Jesus would have accepted that definition. He certainly seemed to model it. The disciples learned their lessons from a teacher on the move. He was healing, working with the poor, interacting with the people of His country, and touching the untouchables. And then, after providing an ongoing example for His disciples, Jesus sent them out on a similar mission. They had the opportunity to succeed or fail on their own before retreating to the Master for further lessons in righteous action.

Real religion, said William Penn, does not take men out of the world but puts them into it, in the hope of bettering it. [11] What is true of Penn's "real religion" is just as true with Jesus' real education. It is an education with the end product of mission, movement, and labor for the kingdom of God on this earth.

When suggesting to the evangelical world that Jesus taught His disciples for the purpose of redemptive action and that such a purpose must be applied to our current situation, some people squawk, "Works righteousness!" This is nonsense. A proper understanding of Scripture reveals that there is nothing we can do to earn our salvation. On the other hand, when we allow God to do in us what He wants to do, then we will have a faith that is necessarily evidenced by works.

In support of that position, we might look to the Book of James, pulling out verses such as those in the second chapter of his pragmatic book, "Faith, if it has no works, is dead, being by itself . . . are you willing to recognize, you foolish fellow, that faith without works is useless? . . . you see that a man is justified by works, and not by faith alone . . . faith without works is dead" (vv. 17, 20, 24, 26). Ephesians 2:8-10 speaks to the same concerns: "For by grace you have been saved through faith; and that not of yourselves, it is the gift of God; not as a result of works, that no one should boast. For we are His workmanship, created in Christ Jesus for good works."

Those are powerful passages. But even more striking, in my estimation, are those verses vividly brought to life in the ministry and teaching of the Rabbi Jesus. Faith and works, in the belief and actions of Jesus, are too closely intertwined to be separated. They are necessarily wed.

Jesus was an activated teacher for several reasons, not the least of these being a world in desperate need. He inaugurated His public ministry in the synagogue of Nazareth by reading and commenting upon those familiar verses in the Book of Isaiah: "The Spirit of the Lord is upon me, because He anointed me to preach the Gospel to the poor, He has sent me to proclaim release to the captives. And recovery of sight to the blind, to set free those who are downtrodden, to proclaim the favorable year of the Lord" (Luke 4:18-19).

Some try to spiritualize these words, suggesting that it is the spiritually poor, captive, blind, and downtrodden for whom He came. No doubt that there are plenty of other passages that point to this aspect of Jesus' ministry. Yet the preceding verses and Jesus' subsequent address make clear that He personally fulfilled them. And His life reflected the truth of that claim in more than a strictly spiritual sense. Ron Sider writes this about Jesus: "He spent most of His time not among the rich and powerful in Jersualem, but among the poor in the cultural and economic backwater of Galilee. He healed the sick and blind. He fed the hungry. And He warned His followers in the strongest possible words that those who do not feed the hungry, clothe the naked, and visit the prisoners will experience eternal damnation" (Matt. 25:31-46)."[12]

There were severe needs in Jesus' world, and He intended that His disciples be trained via living example to meet them. Further, they were to perpetuate a movement that met those needs. A look at early Christian documents reveals no real surprises in this area. Take the following testimony from the Christian philosopher Aristides (A.D. 125) as an example:

They live in awareness of their smallness. Kindliness is their nature. There is no falsehood found among them. They love one another. They do not neglect widows. Orphans they rescue from those who are cruel to them. Every one of them who has anything gives ungrudgingly to the one who has nothing. If they see a traveling stranger they bring him under their roof. . . . If one of them sees that one of their poor must leave this world, he provides for his burial as well as he can. And if they hear that one of them is imprisoned or oppressed by their opponents for the sake of their Christ's name, all of them take care of all his needs. . . . If anyone among them is poor or comes into want while they themselves have nothing to spare, they fast two or three days for him. In this way they can supply any poor man with the food he needs. They are ready to give up their lives for Christ, for they observe the words of their Christ with much care. Their life is one of consecration and justice, as the Lord their God commanded them.[13]

Christ called His disciples and trained them to respond to people's needs. Certainly that benefits the needy person; but the other benefactor is the serving disciple. Made in the image of God, we have a built-in need to serve, to reach out, and to help others. It is a common assertion that love by definition must be outgoing if it is to be love at all. It is not something you can keep to yourself; it must be poured out before it can be truly experienced. Paul Brand recounts an encounter with a

French monk that illustrates how desperately the human spirit needs to serve.

Abbe Pierre was a Catholic friar who was assigned to work among the beggars in Paris during World War II. Convinced that these beggars would have to mobilize themselves for action if their plight was to improve, he decided to teach them how to do their jobs better. They systematically scoured the city to collect the bottles and rags which they had formerly sought sporadically. They built a warehouse from discarded bricks and started a business in which they sorted used bottles from hotels and businesses. But Pierre's project really began to know success when each beggar was inspired to care for a beggar poorer than himself. An organization, "Emmaus," was formed to continue the budding idea and lend it organizational stability.

A crisis had dawned for the organization, however. Abbe Pierre related to Brand that the work had been so successful that there were now no more beggars left to help in that French city. "I must find somebody for my beggars to help!" he related desperately. "If I don't find people worse off than my beggars this movement could turn inward. They'll become a powerful, rich organization and the whole spiritual impact will be lost! They'll have no one to serve."[14]

Pierre's analysis of his situation is revealing. Spirituality can only be maintained as it is expressed in service to others. It was Jesus' objective to move holy character into the arenas of life where it belonged. To allow holiness of heart and life to be penned up in self-serving occupation was a contradiction to the very God-movement He desired to propagate.

Action That Provides Relevance

The world needs our teaching applied, and our spiritual health is contingent in large part upon such application. An activated faith—Christianity sincerely believed and lived—provides relevance for both its adherents and the onlookers of the world. And the world evaluates any belief system according to its relevance. We must attempt to keep in step with the needs of those we desire to communicate to. Scratching where it itches is what good teaching is all about.

Hathaway Struthers of Columbia Bible College teaches a class on discipleship that covers all the basic doctrines of Scripture. Struthers notes that for such instruction to have optimum impact it must be intentionally practical in nature. "I sometimes ask a question like this," Struthers relates. "We have just discussed the deity of Christ, and I am talking to a married man. What good is this knowledge that Christ is God at four o'clock in the morning if your baby has a temperature of 104 degrees? What good does the knowledge of Christ's deity have to do in that situation?"

It is a good question. Is our faith germane to our current problems?

The great C.H. Spurgeon lays bare the shortcoming of irrelevancy in our teaching:

> . . . the great problems of sublapsarianism and supralapsarianism, the trenchant debates concerning eternal filiation, the earnest dispute concerning the double procession, and the pre- and post-millenarian schemes, however important some may deem them, are practically of very little concern to that godly widow woman, with seven children to support by her needle. . . . I know a minister who is great upon the ten toes of the beast, the four faces of the cherubim, the mystical meaning of the badgers' skins, and the typical bearing of the staves of the ark, and the windows of Solomon's temple: but the sins of business men, the temptations of the times, and the needs of the age, he scarcely ever touches upon.[15]

Does our faith affect our response to the poor and disenfranchised? Does it matter in adultery and divorce? Does it provide answers for the threat of nuclear destruction? Is it relevant to the issue of abortion? What does Christianity have to do with psychological and emotional problems, or famine in Ethiopia, or molestation in the nuclear family? If it matters in these instances, then it will matter not only in our Sunday School lessons about these and other concerns, but also in our actions and reactions to these situations. Said one contemporary teacher, "If you cannot make connections, then what is life all about? Who wants to learn only for knowledge's sake?"[16]

It was Luther who remarked that if you are not applying the Gospel of Christ to the specific problems of your age, then you are not communicating the Gospel at all. Merely talking about the problems will not suffice. We must resist the temptation to deliver mere diatribes on pressing issues and begin instead to deliver redemptive answers and actions. As Richard Foster reminds us, our "Sunday School classes need to hear the whimpering cry of the poor. We are . . . soft on justice. . . . May Jesus Christ, our ever present Teacher, continue to instruct us in how to *apply* His life-giving Gospel to every institution and structure in human society."[17] To refuse His instruction and yet feel that we are somehow embracing the Christian religion is to become, as Millard Fuller suggests, parrots who have learned to chirp "I love Jesus, I love Jesus" without having an inward and outward reality that keeps us moving for the kingdom.[18]

Can we interest people in a Gospel that means working with those who need us most? Will people pause long enough to listen to a message that demands of them such redemptive action—a Gospel, in essence, that requires that they roll up their sleeves and sweat for the answer to human needs? Not all will. Not all did in Jesus' day. There were many potential students who refused His curriculum of learning and spiritual growth. But for those who are willing, the effect for God can be awesome.

Dr. Martin Marty of the University of Chicago pulled no punches in describing contemporary evangelicalism in the *Wall Street Journal* some years back. "If you're part of the evangelical subculture," he said, "it's your whole life. . . . you go to church, you buy religious books, you watch the television programs. But if you're not part of the subculture, you never know it exists."[19] Those words are haunting to me. "You never know it exists." Christianity declared essentially irrelevant because of selfish inwardness that sucks life from a movement that is called to be outward bound. The subtitles of the *Journal* article reflect the author's findings:

> *An Evangelical Revival Is Sweeping the Nation:*
> *But with Little Effect*
> *Shunning the Sinful World*
> *Effect Has Been Small*
> *Shying from Involvement*

For an educator all these headlines are painful, but particularly the last one. Education without involvement is a virtual contradiction in terms when we use Jesus as our standard. As evangelicals, our calling is to become radically involved in the world around us. If we refuse, we will be rightfully branded as the irrelevant movement we have become.

There is the story about a holy man meditating under a tree whose roots stretched out over a river. While pondering his spiritual themes for the morning, he noticed a scorpion caught in the roots, destined to drown in the rising current of the river. Without hesitation he uncrossed his legs and rose to help. He crawled out on the roots and reached down to free the scorpion. Not surprisingly, the scorpion struck back at him every time his hand reached out to help. Someone, hiking by, couldn't help seeing the action of the holy man and scolded, "Don't you know that that is a scorpion, and it is the nature of a scorpion to strike back and sting!" To which the holy man replied, "That is true, but it is my nature to save, and must I change my nature because the scorpion does not change its nature?"[20]

The student of Jesus learns to crawl out on a limb for the world: to love, to reach out, to save. Jesus made sure that He modeled and trained His disciples for that kind of activity. He then commissioned them to go about making the Good News relevant to a hurting and lost world. That is a good education indeed.

The movement of God on earth that began in Genesis, proceeded through Jesus, and was mounted upon the shoulders of the disciples was dependent upon redemptive activity, and through that activity was made ever so relevant to a world in need of divine answers. The Good News was more than good views. It was a redemptive movement on behalf of the Father, Son, and Holy Spirit. The nature of our efforts at Christian education should reflect the pattern of Jesus—one who taught *with* action *for* action. Only then will the Gospel be truly relevant to believers as well as to those looking for a reason to believe.

Beginning Steps . . .

1. *Summarize the primary thrust of your current unit of study. Plan one class outing or project, preferably service-oriented or hands-on experience, which reinforces that objective.*

2. *Parents, jot down the questions your children ask during the course of several days. There will be many! Explore the inherent and heaven-sent possibilities for learning about God, themselves, others, and the world.*

3. *The learning process is incomplete without an application of the information. In your next lesson, either assign a response activity or guide your students in identifying specific ways they can put their new knowledge to work in the coming week. All the better if the activity is one in which you implement the lesson together.*

I'm a self-made man. But I think if I had it to do over again, I'd call in someone else.
—**Roland Young**

As iron sharpens iron, so one man sharpens another.
—**The Book of Proverbs**

Learning Is Best Achieved When...

▶ Students interact together in a variety of settings,
▶ Movement toward objectives and intimate relationships are effectively intertwined,
▶ The stark realities of community are understood and struggled through.

CHAPTER SIX

SHARPENING ONE ANOTHER: THE LEARNING COMMUNITY

George Whitefield once accosted the Rev. John Pool in a friendly manner and gently challenged him. "Well, John," said the memorable preacher, "art thou still a Wesleyan?" Pool proudly straightened as he said, "Yes, sir, and I thank God that I have the privilege of being in connection with him, and one of his preachers." "John," admitted Whitefield in characteristically humble fashion, "thou art in the right place. My Brother Wesley acted wisely—the souls that were awakened under his ministry he joined in class, and thus preserved the fruit of his labor. This I neglected, and my people are a rope of sand."[1]

Whitefield may have been overly self-denigrating, but the point is well taken. Togetherness in loving and sharpening relationship is vital to the preservation and perpetuation of Christianity in any age. A lack of true Christian community threatens to weaken and undermine the educational process. We would be wise to implement, as have all powerful movements of Christian influence, practical patterns of corporate learning which reflect the method of the Master Teacher.

One of the marks of a great teacher is the willingness to afford students the opportunity to learn from each other. If teacher-to-student communication could be represented as vertical transmission, then student-to-student interaction might be termed as lateral transmission. The latter focuses on students instructing each other through shared experiences. Said one professor: "We make the assumption that the people that come to us are not blank tablets but come with unique personal experiences and areas of depth and insight. We put trust in them that they can help, teach, and share redemptively with one another. In other words we tell students not to pool their emptiness but to come to class and pool their fullness." A good direction, for, as one researcher asserts, constructive lateral relationships "[is] probably an absolute necessity for maximal achievement, socialization, and healthy development."[2]

When the Jewish rabbis of Jesus' day gathered disciples, both the vertical and lateral dynamics were at work. The teacher did, in fact, instruct and relate in what might be termed as the "traditional" teacher-student manner where the teacher is the dominant personality in the educational relationship. But even the rabbis of old knew that the educational process was incomplete unless their students debated, argued, worked, wept, and laughed together. One of my friends, Ray Hundley, a missionary teaching in Colombia, South America, considers it a crucial point in ministry when members of the small groups which he leads begin to look not to him alone for answers, but to each other. Very early in the formation of a group, Hundley emphasizes two words: mutuality and reciprocity. In the end, he suggests, that is what New Testament Christianity should be all about.

Task + Relationships

I've read that a single draft horse can move two tons of weight. But two draft horses, working in tandem, can move well over twenty tons of weight.[3] What an apt illustration of the beauty and power of a community working together toward a common goal. Task and relationship must be closely intertwined if Christian education is to be maximized.

In recent years, managerial research has shown the fundamental necessity of this alliance.[4] I also think the concept can be utilized in education. To show how, the following diagram depicts two major dimensions of productive learning:

Concern for Relational	Concern for Task/Objective
▲ Good feelings and intimacy among participants	▲ Results, achievement, performance, outcome
▲ Teacher wants students to: -be happy -be fulfilled -learn and act based on relationships of trust and mutual respect with teacher and other students	▲ Teacher wants students to: -achieve -get the job(s) done -be efficient -expand influence -accomplish
▲ *Feelings* sought after: = sympathy, under-standing, support, love, closeness	▲ *Results* sought after: = attainment of goals, knowledge gained, activation

A balance of both elements is needed for effective learning. Each quadrant depicted in the chart on page 98 represents a different learning approach.

A "Quad One" educational style is *characterized by minimal effort* for the accomplishment of either worthwhile goals or beneficial relationships. The goal is maintenance, not progress. Many failing church programs reflect this style. Participants do not relate effectively to each other, nor do they accomplish much. It is probably just a matter of time, unless a miracle of sorts occurs, before such a situation fades into oblivion. It meets no one's needs and has no reason to exist. Ben Haden once recalled the University Christian Movement, which in 1968 voted itself out of existence. They posted a sign on the

THE MASTER PLAN OF TEACHING

High		
3. High Task Low Relationship	**4.** High Task High Relationship
1. Low Task Low Relationship	**2.** Low Task High Relationship

TASK →

Low ← RELATIONSHIP → High

doors of the organization's offices at the Interchurch Center in New York City: "Gone out of business . . . didn't know what our business was." They were honest, at least! Diagnose your own group. Give your group a score of 0–3 for each description (0 = nothing like us; 1 = a little like us; 2 = somewhat like us; 3 = very much like us). Total at the end and continue on.

Boring _____
Coldness _____
Constant postponement
  of goals _____
Inattentiveness _____
Lethargic _____
Nonchalant _____
Most students are
  non-contribu-
  tors _____
No student
  ownership _____

Teacher and student:
  apathy _____
  disinterest _____
  lack of ambition _____
  lack of concern _____
  lethargy _____
  neglect _____
Withdrawn students _____
Purposeless _____

TOTAL _____

A "Quad Two" educational style *places a high priority on people* and a low priority on the attainment of goals. Close relationships with an emphasis on good feelings is the object here. "Whatever you do, don't rock the boat!" This approach is not all bad, however, in placing a premium on good relationships. With adjustment—namely a sense of purpose—these relationships can be turned to great kingdom benefit. When activated revival happens in a church it is frequently as people in "Quad Two" situations intentionally choose to wholeheartedly commit themselves to kingdom tasks. Until that decision is made, the group often resembles a poorly organized social club. Do any of these words describe your folks? Grade your group on the 0–3 scale.

Mutual appreciation ____
Congeniality ____
Dislikes:
    arguments ____
    confrontation ____
    controversy ____
    disagreements ____
    debates ____
    disputes ____
    saying "no" ____
Easily hurt ____
Intense desire to be
    highly compatible ____

Overlook internal
    problems ____
Overly sensitive ____
Thrives on:
    approval ____
    comfort, support ____
    compliments ____
    harmony
        at any costs ____

TOTAL ____

A "Quad Three" educational style *emphasizes task,* with performance and results paramount. "Feel good" relationships are not an objective—in fact, they could get in the way of productivity. "Get it done now! Fast! Low cost!" Few churches fit this category because members of "volunteer organizations" usually resist strictly performance-oriented demands. However, I have seen some church leaders and teachers who exhibit this pattern; generally, these high task and accomplishment people begin struggling within the organization because there isn't love and acceptance enough to maintain the foundation necessary for the pursuit of objectives. Evaluate (0-3) the descriptions that fit both the teachers and the students in your group:

Controlling ____
Decisions made for students ____
Expected conformity ____
Expressed dislike among the community ____
Excessive teacher blaming of others ____
impatience ____
order ____
requirements ____
Gives directions, but not reasons ____

Intolerant of student mistakes ____
"Know it all" teacher ____
Low teacher priority to: feelings of students ____
group decisions ____
taking blame ____
Overly demanding ____
Taskmaster teacher ____

TOTAL ____

A "Quad Four Plus" educational style is the ideal. It is a *goal-centered, objective-seeking team approach.* Here, students are interdependent and there is common participation in the process. Priority is placed on both accomplishment of the task at hand and formation of highly satisfying relationships. This approach does not ensure the complete elimination of arguments or problems, or that every objective will be met 100 percent of the time. It does mean that the teacher and students cooperate to achieve the stated goals. This style also features a high degree of student-to-student relationship, characterized by a growing love and respect. Continue to evaluate (0–3) those aspects below which are a part of your learning community:

Agreed upon participation ____

Clear, challenging goals (set by both teachers and students) ____

Confronts disputes openly and quickly ____

Creativity encouraged ____

Disagreement allowed ____

Enjoyable working and learning ____

Enthusiastic teacher and students ____

Group ownership and decisions ____

Open-minded ____

Positive orientation ____

Understood priorities ____

Straightforward ____

Teacher invites perspectives different than own ____

New objectives are frequently discussed ____

Two-way communication (teacher to student *and* vice versa!) ____

Wholesome and enjoyable relationships ____

Work gets completed ____

TOTAL ____

What was your highest score? Quad One, Two, Three, or Four? Ideally, you scored highest in Quad Four (high relationship, high task). However, few groups do and thus have much room for improvement toward a Jesus-like approach. If your orientation is less desirable than you would like for it to be, then perhaps you need to begin brainstorming now to change your direction. Begin today to explain, expose, and exploit the weaknesses you can see in your matrix position and move toward the Quad Four.

One final note about understanding and applying such a grid. Everything asserted above with regard to the four quads could be easily applied to any secular endeavor where the utilization of human resources toward a common objective is an issue. Here is where the model takes a different twist with Jesus and His followers. A third dimension of holiness is added.

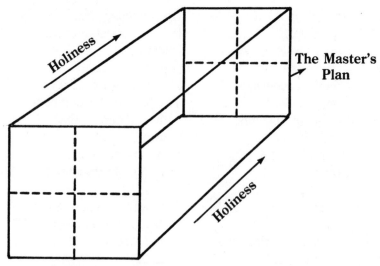

It's not enough to coordinate people and objectives toward worthwhile goals. We desire to submit to holy objectives, the Holy Spirit, the example of the holy Father and Son, and the pursuit of a holy lifestyle. The addition of holiness puts the model on an entirely different plane in pursuit of God and His plan for our lives together.

Knowing where you currently are and starting to gather a group consensus on how to improve are monumental steps in getting where you need to be. If Christlikeness in your educational style is part of your vision, then remind yourself that a learning community in the Jesus tradition is equal to:

HOLY RELATIONSHIPS

+

MOVEMENT TOWARD HOLY OBJECTIVES

The quality of our education increases the deeper in the "Quad Four" area we dare to venture. Taking steps toward that end is vital to our task.

Jesus, in His teaching methodology, sought to develop His disciples as whole persons while continually keeping in mind the task before Him. In the Jesus style of education, the task and relational aspects of Christianity are inextricably intertwined. Building vital relationships involves working together toward a worthwhile goal. Significant accomplishment requires a group of people in action. The key is this: people who redemptively work in love together are learning together. They are developing at the cognitive (intellectual) level, the affective (feeling) level, and the motor (doing) level—from head to heart to hand. A loving and purposeful community is God's goal for His people.

In an early sermon preached by John Winthrop, the first governor of the Massachusetts Bay Colony, the statesman exhorted his fellow colonists with the following words: "We must delight in each other, make others' conditions our own, rejoice together, mourn together, labor and suffer together, always having before our eyes our community as members of the same body."[5] Survival in colonial Massachusetts depended on it. The Christian community that blossomed after Christ's death and resurrection found itself in a similar situation. As a result, they were a "together bunch." Primitive Christianity was a "with-it" religion, and for good reason. Believers had a dynamic relationship not only *with* God but *with* each other. This is dramatically demonstrated in the vocabulary of the Greek New Testament, which contains a whole collection of words beginning with *"sun-."* This prefix denotes the idea of being "together with" somebody else. Some of these words include:

sunaichmalotos	"prisoner with" (Col. 4:10)
sunanakeimai	"reclining at the table with" (Luke 14:10)
sunantilambanai	"bearing with" (Rom. 8:26)
sunarmologeo	"fit together" (Eph. 4:16)
sunbasileo	"reigning together" (2 Tim. 2:2)
sunekdemos	"fellow traveler" (2 Cor. 8:19)
suneklektos	"chosen together with" (1 Peter 5:13)
syzoopoieo	"quickened/made alive with" (Eph. 2:5)
sugkakopatheo	"bear evil treatment along with" (2 Tim. 2:3)
sugkakoucheomai	"endure adversity with" (Heb. 11:5)
sugkatathesis	"agree/consent with" (2 Cor. 6:16)

sugkleronomos	"co-inheritor/fellow heir with" (Rom. 8:17)
summimetes	"fellow imitator of Christ" (Phil. 3:17)
sustoicheo	"stand in line with/correspond to" (Gal. 4:25)
sumpsuchos	"be of one mind with" (Phil. 2:2)[6]

The *sun-* words are unique to the New Testament, appearing nowhere else in classical Greek. Jesus' disciples—and those taught by them—were so affected by the "with-it-ness" of this religion that they had to coin their own vocabulary to accurately communicate their faith and reality. Remarks Dennis Kinlaw, "They repeatedly emphasized that we are in this experieñce of life *with* God, that God is in it *with* us, and that we are in it *with* each other. It is a view that stands in striking contrast to modern individualism" (author's emphasis).[7]

The same kind of community (note: com- stands in our language for the same thing sun- does in Greek—"together" or "with") and mindset make for a terrific environment for education. It could accurately be said that the early Christian believers knew and were known—by God and by each other. That is education at its best. Bertrand Russell reportedly once remarked, "It's co-existence or no-existence." I do not know the context in which this statement was made, but I think it is true on several fronts. In Christianity, it might be said that "It's co-learning or no-learning." If the Christian faith is one of righteousness—that is, right and intimate relationships with both God and man—then co-learning, co-existence, and co-discipleship are essential.

Talk of good relationships usually conjures up images of the warm, cozy feelings of idealized family, or even romantic love. But that is not the only, or even most vital, kind of love. For instance, concomitants of love found in a thesaurus include *admiration, attachment, devotion, sympathy,* and *fellowship.* These terms point toward love as commitment. Other words that are not direct concomitants could accurately be added to the list, words such as *work, struggle,* and *mutual accountability.*

I've heard the following dialogue on more than one occasion:

Disciple:	"Prof, I've come to talk about Fred."
Teacher:	"What is there about Saint Fred you'd like to discuss?"
Disciple:	"Well, for starters, he bugs the daylights out of me!"
Teacher:	"Great! This is really going to allow the opportunity for you to have a truly enriching experience. The thought that has plagued me most since we started this group is that I was silly enough to actually form a group in which everyone got along perfectly."
Disciple:	"Huh?"
Teacher:	"That's right, the last thing we need is matching personalities, identical likes and dislikes, and absolutely no conflicts. I may be a nose, Fred may be a finger on the left hand, and you just might be an armpit. Whatever we are, we're all a part of the body of Christ and we're commanded to love and learn with each other and work as a functioning, caring unit. Your maturity in Christ will deepen as you are able to treat Fred with profound love and respect regardless of your feelings about him as a Christian brother."
Disciple:	"Hmm."

That last murmur is usually a dissatisfied groan. What the disciple usually wants in these cases is either: (1) out of the group, or (2) Fred out of the group, or (3) Fred to start "acting like I want." It's a natural feeling. We all prefer situations where people are like us—laugh at the same things, enjoy the same ball teams, and have the same interests—but that is not how 99 percent of Christian relationships work. Maximum learning comes through maximum righteous adjustment to relationships—whether they are pleasing alliances or not. God places other people in our lives so that we might learn from them, regardless of whether or not we would have chosen their presence. In fact, being surrounded by people who think and act just as we do could be disastrous.

Some think that Jesus had such a perspective in mind when He gathered His twelve disciples. He aimed for a complementary "sharpening" community. In *The College of the Apostles,* James Vance speculates that Jesus chose twelve different character types—"a picture gallery" of character—in order that His disciples might sharpen one another. In fact, he goes so far as to assert that when sent out two-by-two on their missionary journey each man was matched with a complementary apostolic comrade.[8]

Peter the extremist went
  forth . . .

  with Andrew the conservative

James the elder . . .

  with John the youth

Philip the dullard . . .

  with Bartholomew the sage

Thomas the man of
  doubts . . .

  with Matthew the man of strong
  convictions

James the champion of
  duty . . .

  with Jude the champion of doctrine

Simon the zealot . . .

  with Judas the traitor

That Vance is correct in his particular matchings is debatable at best, but the spirit of his theory coincides with the principle of disciple interaction and its pedagogical value.

Today I shared a meal with a middle-aged pastor from the

community and a young seminary student, who together with me, constitute a small discipleship group. The discussion turned to the King James Version of the Bible (always a volatile topic at evangelical seminaries!). One of my friends thought it outdated, the other used it every day for personal devotions and preaching and solemnly vowed to do so for the remainder of his ministry. Here were two different personalities, two different seasons of life, two different perspectives arguing over which version of the Bible is superior. It was not a life-shaking matter but an interesting dialogue nonetheless. I had plenty to say on the topic, but I felt the Spirit nudge me aside from the friendly disagreement, to enter only when I could help guide and clarify the discussion. It proceeded quite well, by the way, without the group leader dominating the conversation. By the end of the debate, when conversation quickly turned toward the topic of fudge brownies, a wealth of insight and viewpoints had been shared. In short, no notes were taken, no teacher had lectured, no charts or graphs were flashed on the wall. But we had learned—about each other, the variety of angles to a subject, and the process of intelligent interaction. Few opinions changed, but our minds and hearts were stretched because we allowed those differences to sharpen our lives.

Lessons are learned, without a doubt, through teacher to student interaction in formal classroom arenas or education. But of no less impact is:

▲ The meal in the cafeteria following class, where perspectives and viewpoints are shared in lively discussion among students of the Gospel.

▲ The pupil vigorously debating on the way out of Sunday School class about which is more important—evangelism or social action.

▲ The lay worker laboring to bring a wholistic program of "the Good News" to a nursing home in their area.

▲ A Bible study group working through personality conflicts in order to more effectively relate to and learn from one another.

▲ A walk in the park where one contemporary disciple shares a struggle in her life with a fellow pilgrim from her church.

▲ A racquetball game where students sweat together and gain insight into each other's backhand and temperament.

One of my professors in seminary, picking up on this idea, scheduled a discipleship class that met twice a week — once for classroom work and the other for a pickup game of basketball. Asked why he limited the class to seven men, he announced that he was the eighth "and that made four people per team!" He continued, "I arranged for the gym two hours a week, and I would go over and we would work out. There are some things you can do better playing ball than you can do in a prayer meeting." A few of my friends saw some of these games. They played, each side, to win. Sweat, pick and rolls, flares of temper, laughter; but most of all, growth. Students and professor learned from each other with shoes squeaking and elbows flying. Disciples were made as they sharpened one another, through physical fitness, for the kingdom.

We learn as we go, as we struggle, as we relate. It would be foolish for an educator to discount such avenues of growth.

The Collective Mind

For the most part, if we are intent on learning within a God-directed community, we will find ourselves much more apt to be successful in our decisions. I have often yearned for the interaction which, I understand, has characterized certain Quaker communities. Richard Foster recounts the story of two people who came before one of the Quaker fellowships with which he was associated, requesting the counsel of the church concerning their engagement and impending marriage. With a gentle spirit of prayer, the group sought the mind of God on this vital matter. With compassion and unity they voiced *their corporate sense* to the couple that at that time marriage would be unwise. The couple postponed, then later decided against, marriage. "Time," says Richard Foster, "has demonstrated the wisdom of their decision."[9]

The Church of the Saviour in Washington, D.C., cultivates a similar approach. Any member who feels that God is leading him to establish a mission group or to initiate a certain outreach "sounds the call." The individual then shares, at a meeting of the congregation, the vision. Interested persons may join together to pray, question, search, and generally "test the call." The eventual counsel of the small group determines whether the vision should be pursued, abandoned, or tabled until a later date. Some in the group may choose to band together to establish that vision as part of the ongoing life of the Church.[10] The point is that a learner and activist seeks out other disciples to discover the will of God and sharpen the vision of their lives — together.

"Iron sharpening iron" has roots in church history as well. In the *Little Flowers of St. Francis*, Brother Ugolino tells how St. Francis of Assisi held community in high esteem. Francis wondered "whether to give himself only to continual prayer or to preach sometimes." He wanted very much to know which of these would "please our Lord Jesus Christ most." How to know? He sent Brother Masseo to request that Sister Clare and Brother Silvester "pray devoutly to God . . . that He may deign to show me what is best. . . ." Brother Masseo therefore returned to St. Francis. And the Saint received him with great charity: he washed his feet and prepared a meal for him. After he had eaten, St. Francis called Brother Masseo into the woods. There he knelt down before Brother Masseo, and baring his head and crossing his arms, St. Francis asked him: "What does my Lord Jesus Christ order me to do?"

The answer was a corporate response:

Brother Masseo replied that Christ had answered both Brother Silvester and Sister Clare and her companion and revealed that "He wants you to go about the world preaching, because God did not call you for yourself alone but also for the salvation of others."

And then the hand of the Lord came over St. Francis. As soon as he heard this answer and thereby knew the will of Christ, he got to his feet, all aflame with divine power, and said to Brother Masseo with great fervor: "So let's go—in the name of the Lord!"[11]

St. Francis understood this simple concept: corporately learning and seeking the will of the Lord is infinitely more powerful than individualistic pursuit. This is true whether the matter is prayer or the study of books. The Jewish community recognized this dynamic; one of its sacred writings in the Talmud revealed that community is essential for correct understanding. "Form groups for the purpose of study, for Torah can be acquired only in a group."[12] There is power in a learning community. And if each member of the community is equally intense and sincere in his or her desire to know the truth, the resulting insight brings increased purity.

That "two heads are better than one" can be readily illustrated by the often used simulation exercise entitled "Lost on the Moon." In it, a group of people is given a list of items and asked to prioritize them according to their probable utility. The goal is to get from a crashed spaceship back to the rescue craft some two hundred miles away. The items to be prioritized include:

Box of Matches	——	Food Concentrate	——
Fifty feet of nylon rope	——	Parachute silk	——
Solar-powered portable heating unit	——	Two .45 caliber pistols	——
One case of dehydrated milk	——	Two 100-pound tanks of oxygen	——
Stellar map (of moon's constellation)	——	Self-inflating life raft	——
Magnetic compass	——	Five gallons of water	——
Signal flares	——	First-aid kit containing injection needles	——
Solar-powered FM receiver transmitter	——		

First, participants rank the items as an individual exercise; then, in groups of five to seven. For the group endeavor, members compare results and give the rationale behind their answers in pursuit of a consensus. The goal is to compile the best possible answers. (To learn the answers recommended by experts at NASA's Crew Equipment Research Department, turn to the end of the chapter.)

The lesson of the "Lost on the Moon" exercise is clear. If group efforts are characterized by "truth-seeking" rather than "debate-winning," the average group score almost always exceeds the average individual score. The consensus of a number of individuals who truly seek the better answer is virtually always more accurate. Jay Hall, inventor of the game, made the following observation:

> *I found groups that had improved the most and scored the best consistently tried to get every member involved. They actively sought out the points of disagreement, and thus promoted conflicts, especially in the early stages. The most ineffective groups, on the other hand, tended to use simple decision techniques, such as majority rule, averaging, and bargaining. They seemed to feel a strain toward convergence, as if it were more important to complete the task than to come up with a decision they could all agree on.*[13]

Hall recommends several guidelines to help in consensus-forming within the small group. I include the following:

▲ Avoid arguing for your own rankings. Listen to others carefully before you press your point.
▲ Do not change your mind to avoid conflict. Be suspicious when agreement comes too easily. Yield only to positions that have objective and logically sound foundations.
▲ Differences are natural, expected, and to be sought out. They generally help if used. A wide range of information and opinions will help the group come to a better solution.[14]

There are, of course, exceptions to the rule that majority

opinion is more accurate than individual. We can all probably think of instances where we were extremely pleased that we didn't follow the majority opinion of the collective body. But these are rare exceptions when a group genuinely seeks to find the best avenue of well-being for both the individuals and gathered body involved.

What does all this have to do with implementing the teaching style of Jesus? The "body of Christ," a key concept of Scripture, is not only stated explicitly in the Word but also demonstrated vividly in the teaching style of Jesus. It was a methodology of give and take among the disciples—of arguments, of laughter, of intense discussion, of shared lives. After Jesus ascended into heaven, the effectiveness of such teaching—minus the Teacher—was tested. Although we do not have the full account of how this lesson fleshed itself out in the early Church, glimmers of *koinonia* shine through the story, especially in Acts. The believers met together, prayed together, shared whatever they had, and sought the good of the kingdom and of each other. Frankly, we shouldn't gloss over the fact that there were also vehement arguments. But where the cause of Christ continued to be the focal issue, holy consensus made the best of the conflicts.

Our Creator intends us to be a body, and in such community we best learn, grow, and develop. To a tired and often cynical world, there was—and still is—something strangely beautiful about Christian community that internalizes and acts out the love of Jesus. And those of us on the pilgrimage of faith find that we are better in concert than solo. We were meant to commune with God and with each other.

It Will Take Patience

Authentic Christian community is wonderful, but as with most worthwhile endeavors it is easier said than done—and usually, said and not done. M. Scott Peck describes the growth and development of community as a series of four sequential stages through which individuals move in the process of forming a cohesive group. The stages are: (1) Pseudocommunity, (2) Chaos, (3) Emptiness, and (4) Community.[15] Peck does not insist that all communities necessarily follow this pattern. But many groups do, and to abort this frequently trying process, as tempting as it may be, will result in less than Community (with a capital "C").

Pseudocommunity is that stage of corporate life characterized by an almost utopian feeling. People are together, enjoying one another, and apparently learning together as they move, serve, and absorb new perspectives. But the interaction, though pleasant, is relatively shallow. *Chaos* occurs when things begin to go awry. Lisa gets underneath Bill's skin. Jim disagrees with Joe. Fred, a conservative Republican, finds out that Judy is a liberal Democrat. People begin disagreeing on means to goals, then the goals themselves, and eventually everything in between. Personality conflicts enter into the fray, and it is an amazing revelation to most that this isn't the congenial little group of saints that everyone thought it was going to be, after all.

At times like these we are severely tempted to abort the process. "All I wanted to do was meet some new people" some will roll around in their minds. "I thought this was just going to be a Bible study" says another. "These people are starting to annoy me," thinks someone else, fidgeting through yet another group meeting. "Why can't people," the activist moans, "just do the work of the Lord and be happy?" Different perspectives, backgrounds, and goals emerge whenever a group of people comes together. A number of options present themselves. We can (1) sacrifice goals on the altar of relationships, (2) sacrifice relationships on the altar of goals, (3) maintain less than the best of both, or (4) struggle on to accept and reconcile our differences in relationship to each other and in service to God.

Pseudocommunity ... *Chaos* ... and then *Emptiness.* If a learning community can work through the emptiness phase, it is possible to emerge as a loving, active community of less-than-perfect individuals who have a redemptive effect on their world. *Emptiness* consists of ridding ourselves of hardcore prejudices, expectations, preconceptions, ideologies, preestablished solutions, and the need to control—just some of the

113

barriers which often stand in the way of true community. According to Peck, real emptiness begins to come about when members of a group are willing to remove these barriers and to admit "their own brokenness—their defeats, failures, doubts, fears, inadequacies, and sins. They begin to stop acting as if they 'had it all together' as they reflect on those things they need to empty themselves of."

In this emptiness phase, attention shifts to allowing and helping people to maximize their peculiar gifts for ministry, rather than making everybody fit into a prepackaged mold. Differences become assets instead of liabilities. Commitment to the group, blended with healthy quantities of humor, enables its members to reach the highest expression of fellowship—New Testament *koinonia* or *Community.* Out of struggle comes peace. The final result? A group of folks now called community who can begin to pursue, in earnest, the task before them.

Two major mistakes often prevent groups from reaching this point of Community. First is a lack of definition. What is community? Certainly not just the euphoric joy of togetherness. Nor is it merely meeting needs, either within or without the body of believers. It is a high task, high relationship learning style marked by a quest for Christlike character and service. The second mistake is a lack of perseverance. Learning in community takes work, patience and a long-range, rather than a short-range, view. Too many groups bow out of the process in the "chaos" or "emptiness" stages and either retreat to fruitlessness or disband. Too many of us think that if we don't form into a community of giddy individuals within a week, or a month, or a year that we have to try something else! Could it be that God would have us strive for His best for two weeks, four months, or ten years? Perseverance is key.

Others beside Peck have attempted to define the quest for "community." One frequently used mnemonic device describes the process as:

Forming—*getting the group together.*
Storming—*struggling to make the group a cohesive fellow-*

> *ship that understands and appreciates each other.*
> Norming—*establishing balance and preparing to fulfill the objectives that the group was made for.*
> Performing—*getting to the business you were called to do.*

Whatever description we use, the steps toward true community involve a struggle, albeit a worthwhile one. Rarely does merely gathering the saints together result in love and service. The best of life's gifts are never like that.

One of the keys to developing a right definition of community, and the perseverance necessary to implement it, is the teacher. It is the educator who must highlight both the responsibilities and the trials involved in the process. I have seen a lot of difficulties alleviated by a good teacher suggesting that yes, we have problems, and isn't it great. Interpersonal adversity allows us to learn and grow in ways not possible otherwise. When such adversity is dealt with in the context of common commitment to significant objectives, it is all the more foundational to learning. Groups that genuinely desire to achieve discipleship "Jesus style" should be informed of the steps Peck and others have identified, and be ready to make the necessary preparation to best utilize these inevitable difficulties for the good and the strength of the learning body.

Occasionally I challenge my classes to examine Scripture and see if they observe Peck's four steps at work among Jesus and the disciples. Although the paradigms discussed above are frequently used to describe the group process in the short-term, such as an intensive weekend retreat, students invariably discover that these steps apply not only to contemporary situations but also to Jesus' learning group on a large level. Some data has to be assumed, but one group of students used the Lukan accounts to draw the following parallels to Peck's theory.

Pseudocommunity—the initial calling of the disciples—few apparent problems. The disciples delight in the fellowship with their Master—they receive great teaching, see Him heal, go to parties and meals with Him, and watch Him show up the intimidating religious hypocrites. "This is fun!" they are undoubtedly thinking. (cf. Luke 5:1–19:27)

Chaos—Time heals all wounds, they say, but it causes some, too. The longer the disciples are together, the more they begin rubbing each other the wrong way. There is a bit of grousing among the troops, and a misunderstanding of what Jesus is really trying to accomplish. To the despair of the disciples, Jesus retreats from ministry to legal squabbles, public humiliation and beating, and then a trip to the disgrace of the cross. (cf. Luke 19:28–23:56)

Emptiness—Jesus has died. His disciples have fled, betrayed, and denied Him. There are feelings of anger, genuine fright, and confusion. They have failed their Master and each other. They are empty, and painfully aware of their own shortcomings. (cf. Luke 22:54–23:56)

Community—Jesus rises, the Spirit of God comes in a mighty way and the disciples begin to fully understand His method, means, and overarching purpose. The movement based on the disciples' message becomes known as a loving, moving, reconciling, and serving community unlike anything the world has seen before. (cf. Luke 24; Acts 1–4)

It is also important to note that the dynamic of community includes a natural time of separation, or sometimes dissolution. New interpersonal orientations, visions, and missions develop which necessitate changes in the makeup of the community. This process can be stressful, especially for the teacher or leader, but is usually quite normal. Dr. Linda Phillips-Jones has documented this dynamic in mentor-protege relationships. She suggests that apprentice-type teacher-learner relationships go through the five stages listed below:

1. *Mutual admiration—where mentor and protege have a highly favorable and idealized image of each other.*

2. *Development—signals much growth, largely in the protege but also in the mentor.*
3. *Disillusionment—recognizing shortcomings in each other, wishing the situation were different. I have heard this called the "getting rid of illusions."*
4. *Parting—a move of the protege towards physical independence.*
5. *Transformation—after the parting, the mentor and protege forget each other, or separate as enemies, or begin to know each other on a new level.*[16]

Note in these mentor-protege relationships the same kind of relationship that Jesus had with His disciples, that there is a time of physical parting and establishment of a new and different relationship. Hopefully, this change results in teacher and student knowing and loving each other on a new level. But I suspect that even in Christian relationships the other dynamics in step five often occur. The thing to remember is that "disillusionment," "parting" and "transformation" are natural parts of the educational process and should be treated as such, with an eye toward making the transition as redemptive as possible.

It shouldn't be hard to see how Jesus uses the steps of mutual admiration and development. They are readily apparent in the Gospel accounts. But there came a time when the disciples did in fact grow disillusioned, wondering who in the world this Jesus was after all, and why He didn't use all His powers to save Himself and His movement. The physical parting took place at His crucifixion and was thus externally imposed, but evidently it was a parting that the Teacher had planned and decided to utilize for its fullest advantage. The transformation and new relationship are spelled out in the Book of Acts.

I have interviewed several teachers, asking if, in fact, these steps occur regularly in their relationships with students. Some don't like to admit it, but they do—almost always. In good teacher-student relationships, there is always an attraction, development, the "getting rid of illusions," a parting—whether by necessity (graduation) or desire ("get me out of this relationship!")— and finally the transformation or new kind of relationship. The disillusionment and parting stages are sometimes disheartening and even unpleasant when they occur, but if love, prayer, and genuine respect characterize the relationship even these latter phases almost always have redemptive value.

I had a teacher, for instance, with whom I shared a rich relationship for about three years. The first half of our time together was enjoyable; the latter portion was marked by a richness that comes only out of struggle and perseverance. I preferred the first half to the last half. The mutually appreciative type of relationship we initially enjoyed was wonderful, but as time wore on we began to understand the downside of each other's personalities and lives. In the end I was ready to leave as quickly as possible, and I highly suspect that he was just as glad to usher me out of town. In subsequent years, however, that relationship has been special and we have developed a long-distance friendship that, for my part, has been profitable in indescribable ways.

Several other students were involved as proteges to this mentor. And as the relationships between us and the teacher developed and changed, the student to student dynamic grew, prospered, and disintegrated in parallel fashion. Today some of us are close friends, others are not. Some of us still write, keep in touch, and learn from each other; I can't even get a phone call through to others. One thing is certain—we all seized the opportunity to learn together under the tutelage of this teacher and grew in ways that not even we could have understood at the time. None of us enjoyed the relationship with each other as much as we would have preferred, but all of us grew and are better servants of the Lord today because of this process. We argued, we cried, we ate each other out of house and home, we were almost to fisticuffs on occasion, but most of all we changed. Whatever the faults of the teacher, he had this one thing on the ball: he knew that significant learning after the teaching style of Jesus must take place in community—iron sharpening iron.

I think that I, and we, learned more that last half—in the time of struggle and periodic conflict—than during the initial honeymoon phase. I have to remind myself, even now, that learning doesn't have to be pleasant to be substantial. Jesus' disciples experienced the same process and were better for it. It is demanding, frequently painful, and often exhausts the emotions. But sticking in there when the going gets tough is infinitely worth the effort.

Following the teaching style of Jesus by intentionally cultivating and persevering through learning relationships requires hard work, the infilling of the Spirit of God, and the same kind of endless love that God shows us. But the closer we get to that kind of learning community, the more we will reflect the Almighty.

Community is a high and difficult calling, but well worth the effort. Christian disciples can be made no other way.

Beginning Steps . . .

1. *Determine which "quad" reflects the dominant education style of your small group. (See chart on page 98.) Can you, as a teacher, identify ways to facilitate both relational and task-oriented elements?*

2. *Utilizing the "Lost on the Moon" exercise, introduce your students to the challenges and rewards of learning together.*

3. *Once the preceding step is complete, brainstorm with your class ways to enhance learning through improved group activity.*

THE MASTER PLAN OF TEACHING

"Lost on the Moon"
(Answers)

Box of matches	= 15 (virtually worthless . . . no oxygen on the moon to sustain flame)
Food concentrate	= 4 (Efficient means of supplying energy requirements)
Fifty feet of rope	= 6 (Useful in scaling cliffs, tying injured together)
Parachute silk	= 8 (Protection from sun's rays)
Solar-powered portable heating unit	= 13 (Not needed unless on dark side)
Two 45 caliber pistols	= 11 (Possible means of self-propulsion)
One case of dehydrated Pet milk	= 12 (Bulkier duplication of food concentrate)
Two 100-pound tanks of oxygen	= 1 (Most pressing survival need)
Stellar map (of the moon's constellations)	= 3 (Primary means of navigation)
Self-inflating life raft	= 9 (CO_2 bottle in military raft may be used for propulsion)
Magnetic compass	= 14 (Magnetic field on moon is not polarized, worthless for navigation)
Five gallons of water	= 2 (Replacement for tremendous liquid loss on lighted side)
Signal flares	= 10 (Distress signal when mother ship is sighted)

First-aid kit containing   =   7 (Needles for vitamins, medi-
   injection needles   cines, etc.; will fit
                                    special aperture in NASA
                                    space suits)

Solar-powered FM   =   5 (For communication with
   receiver-transmitter   mother ship)

*Everyone is a potential winner. Some
people are disguised as losers;
don't let their appearances
fool you.*

**—Kenneth Blanchard,
Spencer Johnson**

*I say to you, he who believes in Me, the works
that I do shall he do also; and greater
works than these shall he do.*

—Jesus

Teachers! Recognize that . . .

- ▶ How we act and speak to our students affects their esteem, for good or ill,
- ▶ Students will likely live up, or down, to our expectations for them,
- ▶ Sin depletes potential—be rid of it,
- ▶ Enthusiasm has broad kingdom implications.

CHAPTER SEVEN

INSTILLING CONFIDENCE IN YOUR CORPS

Never underestimate students whose teacher believes in them. Research shows that if genuine confidence is communicated to the learner, the impact can be monumental. We rise to the expectations that our "significant others" have for us.

Too often we have overlooked this particular aspect of Jesus' educational style. To ignore this crucial element, however, is to neglect His approach to human relationships. Consider these words and actions of Jesus, and their ramifications for the self-esteem of His disciples:

▲ "Having summoned His twelve disciples, He gave them authority" (Matt. 10:1).

▲ "And I also say to you that you are Peter, and upon this rock I will build My church; and the gates of Hades shall not overpower it. I will give you the keys of the kingdom of heaven; and whatever you shall bind on earth shall be bound in heaven, and whatever you shall loose on earth shall be loosed in heaven" (Matt. 16:18-19).

▲ "Again I say to you, that if two of you agree on earth about anything that they may ask, it shall be done for them by My Father who is in heaven" (Matt. 18:19).

▲ "Truly I say to you, that you who have followed Me, in the regeneration when the Son of Man will sit on His glorious throne, you also shall sit upon twelve thrones, judging the twelve tribes of Israel" (Matt. 19:28).

▲ (To the Seventy upon their return from a mission) "I was watching Satan fall from heaven like lightning. Behold, I have given you authority to tread upon serpents and scorpions, and over all the power of the enemy, and nothing shall injure you. . . . rejoice that your names are recorded in heaven" (Luke 10:18-20).

▲ "I will give you utterance and wisdom which none of your opponents will be able to resist or refute" (Luke 21:15).

▲ "Truly, truly, I say to you, he who believes in Me, the works that I do shall he do also; and greater works than these shall he do" (John 14:12).

▲ "Greater love has no one than this, that one lay down his life for his friends. You are My friends" (John 15:13-14).

▲ "You will bear witness also, because you have been with me from the beginning" (John 15:27).

▲ "Go therefore and make disciples of all the nations" (Matt. 28:19). "You shall receive power . . . you shall be My witnesses . . . even to the remotest parts of the earth" (Acts 1:8).

From these verses and biblical examples we can derive several conclusions apropos to the Master-disciple relationship.

1. Jesus challenged the disciples to perform at a level totally unfamiliar in their previous experience (a worldwide vision and authoritative impact vs. fishing, tax collecting, etc.)

2. Jesus' attitudes and opinions about the disciples were aimed at positively impacting their self-esteem and performance ("he who believes in Me" . . . "I have given you authority" . . . "you have been with Me from the beginning").

3. The Teacher fully expected, desired, and predicted that the disciples would exceed His own immediate impact ("greater things you shall do" . . . "you shall go to the remotest parts of the earth").

4. Underlying the Gospels, and these verses in particular, is Jesus' belief in His disciples and His continual efforts to relay that confidence to them.

That doesn't mean, of course, that Jesus wasn't a tough task-master or didn't have a few harsh correctives for the disciples. He often did. But those teaching moments of verbal discipline were bracketed by a clearly communicated attitude: (a) I love you, (b) I have an objective for you to accomplish, and (c) with My help, you will succeed and have a kingdom future.

The Roman poet Ovid, who died during Jesus' teenage years, was known for his witty and sophisticated love poems. He frequently recorded tales, taken from popular legends and myths of the time, recounting the adventures and love affairs of various gods and heroes. In what he considered his greatest work, the *Metamorphoses*, Ovid expands on a fascinating piece of myth that showcases a sculptor by the name of Pygmalion. This artist meticulously carved out of ivory a statue representing his ideal of womanhood and did such a masterful job that he could scarcely help but fall in love with his creation. Venus, in answer to the love and prayers of poor Pygmalion, brought the statue suddenly to life. I include a few lines from the story:

The festal day of Venus, known throughout all Cyprus, now had come, and throngs were there to celebrate. There, [before the altar] when his offering had been made . . . he prayed: "If it is true, O gods, that you can give all things, I pray to have as my wife—" but, he did not dare to add "my ivory statue-maid," and said, "One like my ivory—." Venus heard . . .

When he returned, he went directly to his image-maid, bent over her, and kissed her many times . . . and as he kissed, she seemed to gather some warmth from his lips. Again he kissed her; and he felt her breast; the ivory seemed to soften at the touch, and its firm texture yielded to his hand . . .

He is amazed; but stands rejoicing in his doubt; while fearful there is some mistake. . . . It must be flesh! The veins pulsate beneath the careful test of his directed finger. . . . Now real, true to life—the maiden felt the kisses given to her, and blushing, lifted up her timid eyes, so that she saw the light and sky above. . . .

The goddess graced the marriage she had willed. . . . the statue-bride gave birth to her dear daughter Paphos. From which famed event the island takes its name.[1]

Though presented here in abbreviated form, the story of Pygmalion illustrates the miraculous wonders wrought by love and prayer. Several centuries later George Bernard Shaw penned a play, first performed in 1913, based on this classic legend. A phonetics teacher falls in love with his student, a Cockney flower girl, and they end up changing each other's lives. That play is perhaps more commonly known in its musical version, "My Fair Lady." Its lesson is simple but profound. The attitudes and actions of the creator, lover, teacher, and mentor dramatically impact student esteem and performance. That play, adapted to a Broadway musical and movie, contains the following lines: "You see, really and truly . . . the difference between a lady and a flower girl is not how she behaves, but how she's treated. I shall always be a flower girl to Professor Higgins, because he . . . treats me as a flower girl . . . but I know I can be a lady to you because you treat me as a lady, and always will."[2]

This principle of instilled confidence was demonstrated in a famous study conducted at Harvard University by Robert Rosenthal and Lenore Jacobson, the results of which were recorded in a book entitled *Pygmalion in the Classroom*. The study involved several elementary school classrooms. The pupils were given a standardized test which purportedly indicated the presence of some "late bloomers" in the classes of participating teachers. The test results were used to convince those teachers that unusually large achievement gains could be expected although, in actuality, there was no real reason to expect such gains. Achievement test data at the end of the year (eight months later) showed that the "bloomers" had indeed turned in performances surpassing those of their classmates. The reasoning? Teachers, when they expected greater things from students, acted accordingly and thus fostered higher achievement. Overenthusiastic reports of this study have often been used to show that "wishing can make it so." This conclusion, of course, is highly optimistic and usually considered terribly naive. But teachers, take note: "our expectations do affect the way we behave in situations, and the way we behave affects how other people respond."[3]

The principle works for good or ill. One of my friends sat teary-eyed in an early grade school classroom and heard her teacher say, "Kids, don't be like Denise, she asks too many questions!" My friend sadly notes that moment in time, and in retrospect, its detrimental effect on her whole life.

Another instance of ill: Malcolm X, before he had become the militant black leader, approached a Mr. Ostrowski, whom he had grown to appreciate, and remarked to him that he wanted to become a lawyer. Malcolm X recalls that Mr. Ostrowski looked surprised. He kind of half-smiled and said, "Malcolm, one of life's first needs is for us to be realistic. Don't misunderstand me now. We all here like you, you know that. But you've got to be realistic about being a nigger. A lawyer—that's no realistic goal for a nigger. You need to think about something you *can* be."[4]

Something changed in Malcolm X at that critical point. Anger flowed. He became a Black Muslim. His was to be a piercing, resentful, revolutionary voice. And it was a teacher who was pivotal.

What beauty, however, when the "Pygmalion effect" works for good. Fred Craddock tells a story that illustrates how our behavior toward others profoundly affects self-perception. Vacationing in Tennessee, he and his wife were seated in a restaurant in Gatlinburg when an elderly gentleman sat down and began asking a few perfunctory questions: "How are you? Having a good time? What do you do for a living?" Craddock, answered the questions but decided to end the conversation with suggesting that his "living" was made as a "professor of homiletics." Those of us who are clergy know that such answers are terrific for ending all unwanted conversations.

The old man wasn't fazed. "Oh," he said, "you're a preacher! Let me tell you a preacher story." Craddock waited too long to object, because the old man had already drawn up a chair and started to let loose with his tale.

He said, "I was an illegitimate child and never knew who my father was, and that was hard. The boys at school called me names and made fun of me. When I walked down the main street of our little town, I just knew people were staring at me and asking themselves the question, 'I wonder who the father of that boy is?'

"One day a new preacher came to town and everybody was talking about how good he was. I had never gone to church before, but one Sunday I decided to go and hear him. He was good and I kept going back. But each time I would go late and leave early so I wouldn't have to talk to anybody. Then, one Sunday, I got so caught up in the preachers' sermon that I forgot to leave, and before I knew what was happening, he had said the benediction and the service was over. I tried to get out of the church, but people had already filled up the aisles and I couldn't get past.

"Suddenly, I felt a heavy hand on my shoulder. I turned, looked, and there was that big tall preacher looking down at me and asking, 'What's your name, boy? Whose son are you?' I just shook when he asked that question. But before I could say anything, he said, 'I know who you are. I know who your family is. There's a distinct family resemblance. Why, you're a son of God!'

"You know mister, those words changed my life."

The old man got up and left, and a waitress came over and asked the Craddocks, "You know who that was?"

"No," answered Craddock.

"That's Ben Hooper. Two-term governor of Tennessee."[5]

When I think of these and similar instances, I am forever drawn back to this teaching aspect as demonstrated by Jesus. My perception from Scripture is that He believed intensely in His proteges. Such faith was communicated as He interacted with His disciples, individually and collectively. In the context of *agape* love, He was infinitely optimistic, profoundly reassuring, always thinking and hoping the best for His beloved. The future, in Jesus' eyes, was the disciples'. It was obviously His opinion that they should know that and believe it. When Jesus said "I will make you" into something of infinite value, they heard words and felt love such as they had never experienced before in their lives.

It is said that Michelangelo could gaze at a piece of stone— even a cast–off piece—and see the beautiful form that lay within, awaiting his masterful touch. The Pieta, perhaps his most magnificent creation, is said to be the product of a rejected stone. That is true art, seeing the beautiful in the imperfect. In this sense, teaching is an art form. The teacher fashions, as Jesus did with His disciples through loving words and actions, something of marvelous worth. As the Gaither song goes: "Something beautiful, something good/All my confusion, He understood/All I had to offer Him/Was brokenness and strife/But He made something beautiful of my life."

This does not mean Jesus was all winks and smiles in His relationship with His closest associates. Quite the contrary, there were times when He grew frustrated with their obtuseness. On occasion He had to openly rebuke them. One of the most stunning of these was when Jesus revealed His impending suffering and death. Peter took the Master aside to rebuke Him, flatly denying that such a thing could come about. Jesus' reply? "Get behind Me, Satan! You are a stumbling block to Me; for you are not setting your mind on God's interests, but man's" (Matt. 16:23). What a stinging pronouncement! It must have set Peter reeling. But Jesus knew that Peter had to learn the priority of obedience to God's plans, not man's designs. And when the event did finally come about, and Jesus was arrested in the garden, He again had to chastise His irrepressible companion. When Peter pulled a sword on the high priest's slave and whacked off his ear, Jesus responded, "Stop! No more of this" (Luke 22:51). In Matthew's account He goes on to say, "Put your sword back into its place; for all those who take up the sword shall perish by the sword. Or do you think that I cannot appeal to My Father, and He will at once put at My disposal more than twelve legions of angels?" (Matt. 26:52-53). Jesus then demonstrated a radically different attitude by healing the oppressor whom Peter had opposed. And after Peter, who hotly protested that he would not, denied Jesus the third time, Luke tells us that "the Lord turned and looked at Peter" (Luke 22:61-62). No words were exchanged but the sad, perhaps disappointed, gaze of Jesus apparently had great effect, for Peter "went outside and wept bitterly."

Peter wasn't the only target of Christ's correction. For instance, when a Samaritan village made Jesus unwelcome, James and John proposed commanding fire to come down from heaven to burn up the inhospitable residents. "But He turned and rebuked them" (Luke 9:55). And the disciples as a group came under fire when they took to task those who brought the children to Jesus to be blessed. Jesus was indignant at their behavior and told them so; then He took the children and blessed them. Jesus knew the great potential of the disciples to succeed. But He didn't deny their potential to fail. He was realistic about the debilitating effect of sin in the forms of pride, doubt, lack of compassion, and other damaging attitudes, actions, and decisions of the will. He warned and rebuked them so that they would be aware of personal pitfalls and correct the problems. He knew that willful sin wouldn't simply diminish the disciples' effectiveness for the kingdom; it would decimate their spiritual power.

One way to illustrate the disabling power of sin is with the mathematical formula discovered by German physicist Georg Ohm in 1826. Ohm's Law, which describes the physical properties of electricity, simply states that current at the point of use is equal to the force at the source divided by the resistance in the channel through which it flows. It looks like this:[6]

$$\frac{\text{current at point}}{\text{of use}} = \frac{\text{power source}}{\text{resistance}}$$

Apply this law to Christian living and education and you can begin to see the potential effect of sin upon our lives.

$$\text{A Holy Life} = \frac{\text{my potential as a Christlike human}}{\text{sin: pride, willful disobedience against God, damaging attitudes, etc.}}$$

Think about this for a moment. If a person has holy potential of one hundred units yet holds just ten units of sin in whatever form, that gives him a "holy life quotient" of ten.

$$\text{Holy Life Quotient} = \frac{\text{"Holy Potential"} = 100}{\text{"Units of Sin"} = 10} = \frac{100}{10} = 10$$

If Ohm's law has any correspondence to the spiritual, then we tend to level ourselves off to the lowest common denominator. It is undoubtedly odd to think and figure in such terms, but suffice it to say that sin is not something which merely *subtracts* from Christian living; it operates on the principle of *division* to dramatically diminish the effect of our lives for God's kingdom. Sin creates a disproportionate resistance to Christian growth and service. If we as teachers love our students, can we allow such resistance to go unchecked? Jesus didn't think so. Neither must we.

We can't help but notice, however, a frustrating difference between ourselves and Jesus when trying to emulate this aspect of His teaching ministry. Simply put: He was sinless. We are sinful, even as Christian teachers, leaders, and guides. How can we hope to help our students overcome this menace to their potential for Christ when we struggle with the same things?

We err if we resign ourselves to the inevitability of sin and leave the matter at that. What can we do? Item One: we should attempt to make ourselves accountable to a group of other believers who can help us take the sin in our lives seriously. The early Methodists used to gather in band meetings and ask each other questions along this line. "Do you desire to be told of your faults?" "Do you desire that every one of us should tell you, from time to time, whatsoever is in his heart concerning you . . . whatsoever we think, whatsoever we fear, whatsoever we hear, concerning you?" The basic idea was to open yourself up to people who loved you and wanted to sharpen you for the kingdom. This accountability principle can work if we earnestly desire to get serious about the sin issue.

Once, while completing some research in the library, I came upon a copy of Thomas Jefferson's Bible. It was unlike any I had ever seen. This founding father of our nation had taken a normal Bible and clipped from it all the verses he did not like. Then he did a paste-up job and renamed the volume "Thomas Jefferson's Bible." At least he was honest! A Deist, Jefferson didn't believe in the miraculous. A few cuts and slices later, there were no miracles and he had a new Bible suited to him. Isn't this what we effectually do in practice by omitting a fundamental tenet of Scripture, such as confessing our sins to one another and seeking restitution for those who have been wronged? Recently, one of our most dynamic evangelical leaders humbly resigned his position in a major parachurch organization because of his involvement in an adulterous relationship. He noted that one of the major pitfalls of his life up to the time of the sinful aberration was a lack of "mutual accountability through personal relationship." Continuing, he added that "We need friendships where one man regularly looks another man in the eye and asks hard questions about our moral life, our lust, our ambitions, our ego."[7] Sin is far too serious a matter to let go consistently unchecked.

If Item One is taking care of sin in our lives, Item Two is

helping others come to grip with it in their lives. We can approach sin in the lives of our proteges if they know, as Jesus' disciples did of Him, that we love and care for them and only want the very best for their lives and futures. Too many preachers and teachers scream from the pulpits about sin without first communicating to their people that this concern springs from a deep set love and affection for them. Sometimes correction requires a certain harsh tone; other times a warm hug and a gentle nudge in another direction do more good. One thing is sure, people can take criticism if they know it comes from a fellow pilgrim and lover of their souls.

Some argue that you should never let your students know of your faults or struggles. Personally, I find it difficult to accept correction from a teacher who eschews accountability in his own life. That does not mean I won't listen to any and all complaints against my character and actions. But it is much easier to combat these weaknesses when the one who offers help is himself admittedly and effectively engaged in his own spiritual warfare.

The bottom line is that sin is serious and attacking it on an interpersonal level and in appropriate fashion can be a positive exercise. We must wage effective war on that which disrupts, corrupts, and undermines true discipleship. The teacher emulating the approach of Jesus will first of all need to address the problem on a personal level, then put himself into loving intimacy with his students to help them eliminate the negative impact of sin in their lives. If this is done in the context of love, concern, and persistence, then the effort will produce the desired effect—a community that approaches with greater strides its godly potential.

Jesus' Belief Displayed

As has been shown, Jesus displayed His belief in the disciples in the most obvious of ways—words. But words alone are normally not sufficient to make an indelible impression on the heart and life of the learner. So, Jesus backed up His verbal affirmation with action.

The first way we see Jesus showing confidence in His disciples was in His initial choice of them as disciples at large, and then as apostles in particular. The call of Jesus was always a personal call—and thereby the insinuation was "I choose you, specifically, to follow Me. Let's live and learn together!" Such an invitation, in rabbinic circles, meant the sharing of a physical journey with the teacher (literally, "Follow Me!") but also entailed obedience and devotion to his person. It should be carefully noted, however, that in rabbinic tradition the students always sought out the teacher. In general, the ministry of Jesus reverses that process as He pursues the disciples and challenges them at His own initiative. Such a move on the part of Jesus must have been momentous in the lives of the disciples for, as many scholars have noted, these were largely unimpressive men. A.B. Bruce notes, for instance, that they were "ignorant, narrow-minded, superstitious, full of Jewish prejudices, misconceptions, and animosities."[8] Robert Coleman adds that they were "a ragged aggregation of souls . . . [who] had all the prejudices of their environment."[9] Other writers and observers of the Gospels seem to agree. These were not the superstars or highly polished and successful entrepeneurs of their age. They were common, working men with plenty of flaws.

Jesus saw in the disciples qualities that few others had ever noticed. The Master identified characteristics in them upon which He could build for larger kingdom work. What were those qualities?

▲ First and foremost, they must have had *hearts for God.* It is assumed that Jesus saw in the men He chose a hunger for spiritual things.

▲ Second, Jesus recognized and cultivated their *availability* for God and for learning. This is evidenced in the disciples' willingness to leave their livelihoods to be with the Master and then continue to pass on His great message.

▲ Next, is the matter of *faithfulness.* Jesus evidently perceived this handful of men as ones who would be faithful to the learning and ministering task.

▲ Last, they were *teachable.* Perhaps that is the most important quality for where it is present, growth and progress are possible. If the disciple is teachable, other things can be developed. As long as a student resists instruction, problems can't be identified and corrected nor potential achieved.

The first letter of each of the characteristics listed above forms the acrostic HAFT.[10] A haft is the handle of a bladed instrument. Notice in Romans 6:13 the word *instrument*. In the Greek it is *hoplon* or, literally, weapon. A sharp weapon, instrument, or person, though it has great potential to help and defend, is virtually useless without a handle.

Jesus saw in His disciples qualities which He loved, as did Pygmalion in his statue. Through love and prayer He brought these men to life—abundant and everlasting life. Even in their unrefined state, He had confidence in the disciples' potential. The handle was there to be grasped, though the instruments needed some honing. And with time, instruction, and care they become weapons—redemptive blades with handles, so to speak—for the cause of the kingdom. The Gospels, in one sense, are the story of how a teacher transformed a handful of ordinary people into workers for a mighty cause. That is the beauty of discipleship and the potential of believing, loving, and trusting in your students.

David and Micki Colfax have gained quite a bit of notoriety lately because of their homeschooling success. For the past decade and a half they have educated their children exclusively through home-based activities rather than the public school system and have proven themselves quite the educators. Grant, their eldest, graduated with honors from Harvard and was the recipient of a Fulbright fellowship. Brothers Drew and Reed also attended Harvard. Youngest son Garth is still at home studying. "Inherited intelligence!" some might assert. If so, two of those sons received that "inheritance" through their adopted parents, since only Grant and Drew are the Colfax's biological children. When asked about their educational philosophy the Colfax educators try to beg off, but eventually admit this single overriding principle: " . . . it is only that children *will* learn, *will* aspire to excellence, if we recognize and respect their different interests and abilities and give them a chance to develop them. In our view, every child is gifted one way or another." Those words are penetrating: "everyone is gifted . . . give them a chance to develop."[11] That is what education should be all about.

The second way that Jesus bolstered disciple esteem was through yoking Himself intimately with them. Notice in the New Testament that when Jesus describes to the disciples the success that awaits them, it is always contingent upon their being yoked to the Trained One. It is very clear throughout their tutelage that they were to have confidence and authority; but never apart from an intimate relationship with Jesus or the Holy Spirit. From the Godhead the disciples received their power, authority, and confidence. Should they believe in themselves? Surely! But only as they were standing on the foundation of a relationship with God in Christ. Their success was contingent upon their submission and obedience to Him.

I remember one chilly evening back in Lawrence, Kansas, when I was preparing to lead a college Bible study in our home. The lesson was to focus on the word *meek* but, to be honest, my study for the evening seemed to lack that certain "punch" that would make it memorable. I began frantically pacing the carpet, searching for the much-needed creative spark to an otherwise undramatic presentation. Suddenly, I spied my trusty tape recorder and an idea flashed across my mind. Recorder in hand, I dashed out the front door, scurried a few blocks down the street, and began to accost whomever I could find with the query, "What does the word *meek* mean to you?" Granted, it was an unscientific survey, but playing the tape back to my Bible study group that evening proved most enlightening. The compiled results are best reflected in the statement of a young man sitting with his girlfriend in a local cafe. "Meek," he declared as he gazed into his brew, "means wimp." The response was a common one. In the eyes of our world, the meek top the list of those least likely to succeed. In this age of the self-centered pursuit of happiness, it is hard to believe that the meek will inherit the earth. Yet that is precisely what Jesus promises.

A closer look at the backdrop of Jesus' culture sheds a bit of light on the word. Meek (*praus*) was commonly used to describe wild animals that had been domesticated—trained, tamed, and otherwise harnessed—so that the savage beast became capable of working profitably alongside man. The image that presents itself in this definition is not lack of energy or strength; rather, power under control. Gerald Mann illustrates this insight with the story from Greek antiquity of a young soldier writing to his sweetheart concerning a gift he longed to present to her: a silver stallion. "He is the most magnificent animal I've ever seen," related the soldier, "but he responds obediently to the slightest command. . . . He allows his master to direct him to his full potential. He is truly a *meek* horse."[12]

Meek is not synonymous with wimp. Elton Trueblood, in fact, named his own worldwide organization—the "Yoke-fellows"—after the strength of the concept meek: "We become trained and disciplined for service only as we are yoked together. Thus, significantly, it is in Christ's clearest call to personal commitment—that in which He says, 'Come unto Me'—that He also says, 'Take My yoke upon you.' The Company of Christ is tied together by Christ's yoke. That is why 'yokefellow' is a synonym for committed Christian. Though the younger generation does not understand it now, every farm child of the early part of our century understood very well that no colt is normally trained alone. It is 'hitched' with one already well trained."[13]

Similarly, fellow Quaker Richard Foster notes that "A horse or ox is trained to work peaceably and well by being yoked or harnessed to one already trained. . . . We too are yoked to One who is trained. Our only task is to keep in step with Him. He chooses the direction and leads the way. As we walk step by step with Him, we soon discover . . . the joyful life of hearing and obeying."[14]

We may have joyful confidence in discipleship and the reproduction of the Life in us because we can be yoked with someone who believes in our infinite capabilities as kingdom educators—that Someone is God Almighty. When we, as teachers, become yoked to an understudy or group of peers,

God in us desires to have that same enabling, encouraging, edifying effect on our students and fellow learners. Initially, people often feel that being so closely associated with a teacher or especially with Christ is too imposing. With that thought in mind, I remember these lines from Lloyd C. Douglas' book *The Robe*. Speaking of Jesus, Marcellus asks Justus, "Where do you think He went?"

> *"I don't know, my friend. I only know that He is alive— and I am always expecting to see Him. Sometimes I feel aware of Him, as if He were close by." Justus smiled faintly, his eyes wet with tears. "It keeps you honest," he went on. "You have no temptation to cheat anyone, or to lie to anyone, or hurt anyone—when, for all you know, Jesus is standing beside you."*
>
> *"I'm afraid I should feel very uncomfortable," remarked Marcellus, "being perpetually watched by some invisible presence."*
>
> *"Not if that presence helped you defend yourself against yourself, Marcellus. It is a great satisfaction to have someone standing by—to keep you at your best."* [15]

Being yoked to Jesus the Teacher was not uncomfortable for the true believers of early Christendom. They knew it could only keep them at their best.

Living into Expectations

While at the University of Pennsylvania, Anthony Campolo posed a question to his Social Problems class that went something like this: "What would Buddha, Muhammad, and the proponents of Mosaic Law say about prostitution?" The discussion was lively and intense and before it was over Campolo moved on to ask the students what they thought Jesus would have said to a prostitute. One of the students answered, "Jesus never met a prostitute."

"Yes, He did," Campolo responded. "I'll show you in the Bible where-"

The student interrupted. "You didn't hear me, Doctor. I

said Jesus never met a prostitute."

Once again Campolo tried to counter by grabbing his New Testament and looking for the appropriate verses to substantiate his position.

"You're not listening to me, Doctor. . . . Do you think that when He looked at Mary Magdalene He saw a prostitute? Do you think He saw whores when He looked at women like her? Doctor, listen to me! Jesus never met a prostitute!"[16]

Jesus expected more than that from those He looked upon. He knew them, what they were meant to be, where they could potentially end up. And many prostitutes, alcoholics, prisoners, and others wallowing in potentially depleting activities were—and are—changed because Jesus looks and sees more than the ordinary teacher sees. He sees saints who can reflect the image of God.

In the late 1970s Marva Collins left the public school system and started her own private school on the West Side of Chicago. It began humbly. Barely a handful of students arrived on the first day of class, so Collins did what she felt most compelled to do—she taught.

Gradually there was an explosion of interest. Her students, black and poor—rejects from the Chicago public school system and labeled everything from "mentally retarded" to "learning disabled"—did away with such traditional educational endeavors as art, music, gym and recess and picked up authors like Dante, Emerson, Dostoyevski and Tolstoy—and all this at early primary school ages. Morley Safer of "60 Minutes," visiting her classroom encountered a 9-year-old who claimed that his favorite author was Geoffrey Chaucer. What's the secret? Collins asserts that "If you believe in children, then all you really need for teaching is a blackboard, books, and a good pair of legs that will last through the day." And she believes it. "Kids can accomplish anything [in her class] because they are not afraid to try." Says one biographer describing her relationship to a particularly difficult little boy: "Eventually, with lots of praise and lots of hugging, his defensiveness would melt. The one thing all children finally wanted was the chance to be accepted for themselves, to feel some sense of self-worth.

Once they felt it, children became addicted to learning, and they had the desire to learn forever."[17]

Let's take a peek into the Marva Collins' classroom:[18]

"I know most of you can't spell your name. You don't know the alphabet, you don't know how to read, you don't know homonyms or how to syllabicate. I promise you that you will. None of you has ever failed. School may have failed you. Well, goodbye to failure, children. Welcome to success. You will read hard books in here and understand what you read. You will write every day so that writing becomes second nature to you. You will memorize a poem every week so that you can train your minds to remember things."

"The first thing we are going to do in here, children, is an awful lot of believing in ourselves."

[trying to get Freddie to take off his coat] "You are so very angry," she murmured gently, "but I know you're not angry with me, because I haven't done anything to you. We all have a good me and a bad me inside us, and I know that you have a good you. Will you help me find it? I'm your friend and I'm going to help you all the time and I'm going to love you all the time. I love you already, and I'm going to love you even when you don't love yourself."

She pulled him close to her, his head resting against her hip. Her long fingers kneaded the tension from his shoulders and stroked the back of his neck. . . . Freddie pushed back into his chair, sat up tall, and with quick, short pulls began popping apart the snaps on his jacket, slipping his arms out of the sleeves. Marva bent over him, balanced his chin on the crook of her finger, and tilted his head back so that he was looking straight at her. The subdued tone of her voice gave way suddenly to a new firmness. "I promise, you are going to do, you are going to produce. I am not going to let you fail."

"Children," she began, "today will decide whether you succeed or fail tomorrow. I promise you, I won't let you fail. I care about you. I love you. You can pay people to teach, but not to care. . . . I don't sit behind a big desk in front of the class. I walk up and down the rows of desks every day and I hug each of you every day."

"I try to make each child feel special. [One] child had a scalp infection and was completely bald. The children at his former school used to throw his hairpiece around the room. Can you imagine any teacher callous enough to let that happen?

"Before he came to my school I told the other children what had happened to him. When he first came to the class we all went to hug him. . . . we kept loving him. Today, I'm happy to see how well adjusted that child is."[19]

The preceding explains the fuss over Marva Collins. From her method and results, it's not hard to understand why she claims, "You have to show that you believe in them—that you know there's nothing they can't do. When I was in public school, some teachers just coasted through the day. They wouldn't take anything home at night but their purses. They'd tell me, 'Why bother? These kids aren't going to learn anything.' Well, they'll learn a lot if you bother."[20]

The lesson from this school teacher on Chicago's West Side is simple. You've got to "bother to believe." It is a process of brainwashing, says Collins' biographer; "brainwashing them into succeeding."[21] An odd way to put it, perhaps, but I think Jesus would approve.

Enthusiasm . . . the God within Us

Of course, the key ingredient in the communication of confidence is enthusiasm. That is what makes Marva Collins great, and it marks most excellent teachers who rise above their peers in the capacity to change lives.

I love our English word enthusiasm. The dictionary discloses that it derives from *en* (in) + *theos* (god). God in us!

Extrapolated to the task of teaching that means transferring an inward God-reality outward. If God is in the business of making us whole and infusing us with heavenly esteem, then we need to make that same process a part of our approach to educating kingdom activists. Marlene LeFever describes a group of self-made millionaires who were asked to list the qualities that had contributed to their success and rate the importance of each.[22] The final tally looked something like this:

Ability	-	5%
Knowledge	-	5%
Discipline	-	10%
Attitude	-	40%
Enthusiasm	-	40%

With these stats in mind, is it any wonder that at Hewlett-Packard, top management's explicit criterion for picking managers is their ability to engender excitement?[23] LeFever, after stating these statistics, poses the question, "How closely, do you suppose, would a successful teacher's percentages match these?" My guess is very closely indeed.

When I was participating on my graduate research team, we wanted to add enthusiasm to our list of effective teaching behaviors but were struggling to accurately define it in behavioral terms. Is enthusiasm identified by voice inflection, mobile facial expression, lots of movement around the classroom, animated gestures—or just what? While discussing possible descriptors, we all became a bit frustrated until somebody in our group suddenly blurted out, "I don't know how to define it, but I darn sure know when somebody has it!"

Dr. Myron L. Fox took his place before an impressive audience of educators and mental health professionals. With style and flair he forcefully addressed his audience on the "mathematical models of memory" and before long they were visibly impressed. His authoritative, witty, and winsome personality won the accolades of that assembly.

From that lecture developed a famous study, for as those present eventually learned, in reality there was no Dr. Fox.

"Fox" was a professional actor asked to assume the identity of a charismatic expert. In actuality, the audience that day had given an incredibly high evaluation to a paid performer—who, by design, uttered deliberate nonsense. Because he had been introduced as Dr. Myron L. Fox and combined an attractive personality with an entertaining message, his hearers gained the impression that "Fox" was an authority with a message for the moment. Few discerned that his speech was nonsense.[24]

"See there," say some who report this study, "it just goes to show you how dangerous enthusiasm can be!" True, there is danger in an unbelievably enthusiastic messenger with a very bad doctrine (a la Adolph Hitler). To loose that communicator on an unsuspecting or undiscerning audience can have disastrous consequences. Enthusiasm, for better or worse, attracts. But the study should not be used to demean effective and attractive delivery. If anything, it should convince us of the power exercised by enthusiastic charm. Paired with the message of Truth, a winsome presentation can enhance receptiveness to the redemptive message. Enthusiasm works and is good. And that enthusiasm, when applied to students, can have profound effect. If it is truly "God in us," that effect will have broad kingdom implications.

Youthworker David Stone recalls listening to a panel of three ministers during spiritual emphasis week at a small Christian college. The question posed to these ministers was simple: "What does it mean to be a Christian?"

The first minister was academic. "Being a Christian," he replied stuffily, "means to acquire knowledge of the Christ through God's Word, developing a ritualistic approach of communication with God and acting on that knowledge with courage."

The next minister was a bit more spiritual in his approach. "To be a Christian is to be washed by the blood of the sacrificial Lamb and cleansed forever in the Temple of the Holy Spirit." With that, he turned to the pastor next to him and asked, "Isn't that right, Brother Bob?"

The youngest of the three ministers was obviously taken aback by the "Brother Bob" inquiry. But he recovered enough to blurt out his feelings. "I'm not sure I know what either one of you said," he began. "When I think of being a Christian, I simply recognize that God loves me and what a tremendous difference that love has made in my life."[25]

Thunderous applause.

Standing ovation.

Jesus loved His disciples. He was enthusiastic about their possibilities. It made a difference. We are called to do the same for our children and students.

Beginning Steps . . .

1. *Who among your students could especially benefit from regular doses of verbal affirmation? List those names on a piece of paper, pray daily for them, and begin practicing on them. Brainstorm several tangible ways that you could, in the very near future, show your belief in and love for them.*

2. *What hopes and dreams do you cherish for your students? Write a credo expressing the positive accomplishments and attributes you expect them to attain and ways to facilitate their progress. This is also a great exercise for both parents and teachers.*

3. *Reflect for a moment on your own life. How are you modeling accountability for your students? Can you identify some areas of struggle? Find someone you trust spiritually and establish an accountability relationship with opportunities for prayer and sharing.*

*Darling, you are not here in this world
for yourself. You have been sent for
others. The world is waiting for you.*
—Catherine Booth
(in her "nightly whisper" to her
sleeping children)

*Whoever wishes to be great among you
shall be your servant, and whoever
wishes to be first among you shall
be your slave; just as the Son
of Man did not come to be
served, but to serve . . .*

—Jesus

Like the Servant Educator, We Must...

▶ Make Christlike choices based on the Servant Model,
▶ Focus primarily on the *needs* of students, not simply wants,
▶ Model a life of servanthood before our students.

CHAPTER EIGHT

THE SERVANT TEACHER

D r. David Thompson, a professor steeped in the scholarship of both the Old and New Testaments, strolled into class one day after all the students were seated and stood in front of us for a long moment before reaching in his pocket for a handkerchief. Hankie in hand, he slowly bent down at the feet of a very startled young man in the first row and began to wipe the dust from his shoes. After what must have seemed like an eternity to the embarrassed student, the professor moved to the next person in the row, and then to his neighbor, carefully polishing the shoes of each one. We all strained our necks trying to see what in the world "Prof" was doing. "Has he flipped his lid?" we thought. "You don't suppose he's going to do this to everybody in class, do you?"

Thompson rose, with flushed face, folded the handkerchief into his pocket, looked at no one in particular and everybody all at once and said simply, "You've got to stoop, to serve."

To be frank, the remainder of that class session is a blur. His lesson for the day dealt primarily with John's Gospel, chapter thirteen—Jesus' washing of the disciples' feet. But the picture of that professor kneeling before his students and shining shoes graphically communicated biblical truth in a way that forever penetrated my heart. Upon reflection, I can't help thinking that Jesus' didactic activity reflected such "stooping activity." He undoubtedly asked the question during His teaching ministry, *"How can I best serve these that God has entrusted to Me? What do I need to do to serve these, My friends?"*

He came to serve. Words penned by Paul from prison to his friends in Philippi describe such a stance: "Do nothing from selfishness or empty conceit, but with humility of mind let each of you regard one another as more important than himself; do not merely look out for your own personal interests, but also for the interests of others. Have this attitude in yourselves which was also in Christ Jesus, who, although He existed in the form of God, did not regard equality with God a thing to be grasped, but emptied Himself, taking the form of a bond-servant, and being made in the likeness of men" (Phil. 2:3-7).

His "servant" philosophy of education frequently differs from ours. We too often prepare lessons and are upset if no one shows up to hear them. He was a lesson and came to help people listen. We desire to teach good students. He yearned to teach to make His students good. We want to know how we can make people fit our pedagogical agenda. He wanted to serve others and bring them to an understanding of God's agenda. We desire maturity in believers so that they might be responsible, "safety-first" adults that fit into our status quo. He desired maturity in believers so that they might be as hungry and eager to learn as idealistic, carefree children. We want to learn and teach to gather in our share of honor, prestige, and power. He sought to lose His life so that others might not be fooled by this world's definition of those things. We crave favorable public opinion. He eventually shunned the affirmation of the masses for the declaration of the truth. We like lessons that feel good and affirm our status. He loved the lessons of God, period. We want to be filled. He said, "Blessed are the poor in spirit" (Matt. 5:3) and desired to be emptied for our sakes. We hold endless seminars on establishing a leadership style in four easy steps! His was an ongoing lesson in sacrificial servanthood. We want to be teachers in a comfortable and well-paid situation. He was a suffering servant/teacher, and comfort or payback was never the overriding issue. Jesus' education is a river based on one overarching goal—to serve those who will in turn serve like Him. Ours often is a swamp—based on a hundred different objectives but no concrete destination. We educate. He is Education. Therein lies the difference.

When I think of such humble stature and the hesitancy of our Christian faith to come to grips with an adequate reflection, I am reminded of Emperor Tiberius musing to himself about this "new Galilean idea" in the novel *The Robe:*

> *"It might be interesting," he went on, talking to himself— "it might be interesting to watch this strange thing develop. If it could go on—the way it seems to be going now— nothing could stop it. But—it won't go on—that way. It will collapse—after a while. Soon as it gets into a strong position. Soon as it gets strong enough to dictate terms. Then it will squabble over its offices and spoils—and grow heady with power and territory. The Christian afoot is a formidable fellow—but—when he becomes prosperous to ride a horse—" Tiberius suddenly broke out in a startling guffaw. "He! he! he!—when he gets a horse! Ho! ho! ho!— a Christian on horseback will be just like any other man on horseback! This Jesus army will have to travel on foot—if it expects to accomplish anything!"[1]*

Lloyd C. Douglas, the writer of these lines, had in mind a great truth. If the Christian faith is to have health, integrity, relevance, and eventual success in its educational mandate, it must be a movement that is content to live, teach, and serve "afoot." Otherwise, we run the sure bet to be just like any other movement gone awry. Jesus, like the above excerpt intimates, began a movement intent and content to stay afoot. To deny a service mandate and mount a horse is to deny the power of our servant example.

The Servant Model
Servant teachers rarely shy away from situations and needs that require attention. Sometimes the needs are simple— chairs to be set up or trash to be picked up. Other times,

someone is hurting—physically, emotionally, or spiritually—and needs a tangible expression of love and concern. Whatever the case, teachers who reflect the Jesus model of living are usually the first to roll up their sleeves and help when an occasion presents itself. And this helping activity is frequently done with students in tow.

It is not enough to lead our students in "How to Be a Servant" Bible studies. We must learn to model service before them. It is an education lifestyle that moves away from the easy chair and TV set. We recognize the need to leave the comfortable homebase and commemorate, through our own experience, Jesus' example as He walked vulnerably and compassionately among the castaways and infirm, the Samaritans, the diseased, and demoniacs.

Charles Colson points out the danger of mere "in-house movement."

> . . . in 1929, when the Soviet government wanted to wipe out the church, what did they do? They passed a law, not to prevent the churches from meeting on Sunday morning, but to make it a crime to conduct church school, to help the poor, to go into the neighborhoods and reach out to people. Believers had to stay within their churches on Sunday morning, and what the Soviet Communists did by decree in 1929, we are allowing to be done to us today by default. [2]

We cannot, as those who seek a Christlike approach to education, default on this issue of service. If we do, we betray an essential part of the Gospel. And we betray our students by neglecting to give them the kind of model that will free them to live as Christ intended.

The Servant Teacher

To be like the Rabbi Jesus, we must stoop to serve as He served. It is an attitude that continually asks, *"How can I best tend to the needs of my people?"* Jesus was willing to go to the limit with such considerations. John 12, one of the most fascinating portions of Scripture I know, illustrates this. In that chapter (v. 20ff), Jesus is approached by "certain Greeks." They came to Jesus, and as the passage suggests, He "answered them." But the question to which He responded is not explicitly stated in these verses. There is a huge gap and an almost eerie silence between the coming of the Greeks and Jesus' answer to their inquiry.

An extrabiblical tradition exists that just may contain a grain of truth. As the story goes, the Prince of Edessa sent emissaries to Jesus asking Him to return with them there. Sensing the danger and death that He would face if He continued His work among the Jews, they begged Jesus to come with them to Greece. In Athens, men's minds were broad and liberal. His teaching would most certainly be appreciated there. Besides, certain peril awaited Him in Jerusalem. Why waste potential years of ministry? Why not escape senseless sacrifice and come where He would be appreciated, live long, have the support of the community, enjoy extended influence, and go down in the history books with "greats" such as Socrates and Aristotle.

Jesus might well have gazed skyward for a moment, pondering their proposal. It wasn't an evil request; in fact, it was quite appealing. There was nothing inherently wrong with a teaching ministry endowed by the Prince. He could enjoy a comfortable life where He was appreciated and His contributions valued. He could make hundreds of disciples through the years. He would go down as one of the greatest who ever lived. Why not Athens? It would be a good choice.

A good choice, perhaps, but not the best. Jesus, after a moment of contemplation, turned to His Greek friends and uttered unforgettable words: "The hour has come for the Son of Man to be glorified. Truly . . . I say to you, unless a grain of wheat falls into the earth and dies, it remains by itself alone; but if it dies, it bears much fruit" (Matt. 12:24).

The group of men seeking this Rabbi perhaps walked away sadly, disappointed that they would have to give the Prince a less than favorable report. But they should have known. A teacher of Jesus' stature and effectiveness could not compromise His calling. Educators who imitate Christ's example serve and sacrifice to accomplish the objectives set for their students.

The servant of God isn't simply after the good opportunity or profitable step up the ladder. No, the servant of God is after the best for those he came to serve. In almost every age, the teacher who chooses the sacrificial best over the glaringly apparent good will be criticized, laughed at, and perhaps even rebuked. That is part of serving. It usually doesn't make much sense to our contemporaries, but it makes a lot of sense to a God who takes pleasure in developing men and women for kingdom living. Such development comes only through a well-placed teacher who is committed to loving, caring for, and serving his or her disciples.

The Servant: The Wise Fool

For those going through high school and college, being a sophomore is rarely a favorite stage. The excitement and newness of the freshman year is over, yet the status of the juniors and seniors is still out of reach. The etymology of that word "sophomore" provides a bit more intrigue. *Sophos* comes from the Greek term meaning wise; *moros* comes from the word meaning fool. Wed to one another, the two terms mean, in the most primitive form, "a wise fool."

There is perhaps no better way to describe the servant-teacher. First of all, he is "foolish" enough to take Jesus' advice to heart. He truly desires to emulate the Master: washing his students' feet, laying down his own life for the lives and careers of his disciples, taking up his cross daily and following after the dreams of God. Let's face it, in the short haul those choices seem rather foolish. Your friends and family, probably just like Jesus', tell you to wake up and be sensible — save your life for something better, go for the gusto, climb the corporate ladder, make some real money, choose a more profitable profession, or set your own agenda.

Several of my friends have been plagued with such a family/friend dilemma. They adopt a life calling that requires a serious deviation from the normal track for persons of their caliber or family and peer orientation. Having made such a sacrificial choice, they then face the nagging rejoinders of their "significant others."

▲ "Why the mission field? Don't you know that you could make a decent living right here in Kansas City?"

▲ "Why a teacher? Everyone knows that is the lowest paid profession known to man!"

▲ "You've got to be kidding! A youth minister? What do you want to do, play games for the rest of your life?"

▲ "Homemaker? Ha! Once you decide to make something of your life, you'll forget that outdated notion."

You do have to be a bit "foolish" in the eyes of this world to teach. But to teach, live, and minister like Jesus—that is something even stranger yet. Still, there are those who seem to have captured this strange spirit of service and sacrifice. Few I can think of top the story of George Washington Carver.

Carver was born near Diamond Grove, Missouri, the son of slaves. His childhood was turbulent. His father was killed and young George was kidnapped, along with his mother and another child. His mother was never located again, but the sickly child was bought back by their "master" in exchange for a $300 horse.

Like many stories of great servants, humble beginnings belied future promise. As a youth, Carver developed a keen mind and sharp intellect, and against overwhelming odds he finally attained bachelor's and master's degrees. Cognizant of his ability, Iowa University offered him a teaching post. It was a coveted position, more so since a black man had rarely before attained such an honored berth. As few of his race had ever been afforded the opportunity, he could finally settle in, engage in serious scholarship and enjoy the comforts accorded his profession.

Then the letter arrived. Signed by Booker T. Washington, it invited Carver to join him in educating the black man in the South. It was a pioneering endeavor, to be sure. He was to head the newly organized department of agriculture at Tuskegee Institute in Alabama. The future was uncertain, the salary considerably less than what Iowa offered, and the trappings of a well-endowed, established institution nonexistent. But what awaited the young scholar was a people and a region that desperately needed him—an eroded, exhausted and parched farmland devastated by poor cultivation practices.

Would he accept? Would he! He traveled southward for a lifetime of sacrifice and years filled with insult from those who refused to accept a black man in their region, regardless of his supposed genius. But he was where he knew he belonged, in a place of service, lifting up a people and a region in desperate need of his expertise. Carver's contributions were legion. He developed ways to add life to the soil through restoration of mineral content and crop diversification. He discovered that peanuts and sweet potatoes produced impressive yields in the Alabama soil. With that knowledge, his next step was to find avenues (over three hundred ways) to utilize these products. In doing so, he revolutionized the economy of the South. His lengthy list of accomplishments included a cross between short-stalk and tall-stalk cotton known as "Carver's hybrid," collaboration with Henry Ford to perfect a process for extracting rubber from the milk of goldenrod, the institution at Tuskegee of a "visiting day" for small farmers to come and learn about soil fertilization, and a "school on wheels" for those unable to make the trip.

Carver, for his servant efforts, became a legend in his own time. Thomas Edison offered the teacher a huge salary—especially in that day—of $100,000 a year and a beautiful new laboratory in which to continue his research. Industry wooed him to engage in various enterprises for increased prestige and monetary gain. Carver shunned them all. Even Booker T. Washington offered to raise his meager starting salary ($1,500) at Tuskegee; Carver dutifully turned it down. His critics thought he was crazy. "Just imagine," they said, "what you could do if you took these jobs, this money, those opportunities. Imagine what you could do for your people!" His reply: "If I had all that money I might forget my people." The epitaph on Carver's grave could have been carved into Jesus' tombstone, had He stayed in the grave long enough for one to be inscribed.

> *He could have added fame and fortune*
> *but cared for neither, he*
> *found happiness and honor*
> *in being helpful*
> *to the world.*[3]

Between Athens and Jerusalem, Carver chose "Jerusalem." All great Christlike teachers do—a sanctified sort of foolishness indeed.

Do we have the mettle to make such choices? Do we have the courage to be so bold?

If being a fool for Christ's sake is a keynote of serving as He served, then the "wisdom aspect" of *sophos/mores* should also be considered. A fool for the sake of the teaching style of Jesus must necessarily approach servanthood with a premium on good judgment and an eye toward the greatest good. It is a state of mind and action that considers not how one can pander after a learner's wants, but how to work hard in pursuit of filling genuine needs. No example of this is more clear than good parenting.

I'm thankful that my folks didn't give me everything I wanted. Had they, my adolescence, for example, would have been full of a candy diet, frequent late nights, money at my immediate disposal, my own set of rules, and stunted growth. As it turned out, my parents fed me what I needed, set curfew, made me earn money for college, set rules that I was expected to live by, and loved me into becoming a whole person. Their attention was on my needs far more than wants, and growth was the result.

Interestingly enough, scholars express the opinion that Jesus utilized a family style of education. He certainly appeared to do so. In other words, like my family, He didn't just allow the disciples to always have what they wanted. He recognized that it wouldn't have been good for them or the broader kingdom. But His finger was certainly upon their needs. For instance,

› The disciples wanted to fish.

›› The Servant equipped them to fish for men and women.

› The disciples enjoyed argumentative jousts about who was the greatest among them.

›› The Servant said that if anyone wants to be first, he shall be last of all.

› The disciples wanted to protect Jesus from children and childish ideas.

›› The Servant taught them to "bring the children unto Me" and reminded the disciples that the kingdom of God belonged to people a lot like them.

› The disciples wanted glory, a few even wanted to sit on His left and right hand in His kingdom.

›› The Servant convinced them they really wanted a cross and a mission, a giving of their lives for the Gospel.

› They expected a political inheritance.

›› The Servant wanted more than the kingdoms of man for His loved ones; He wanted them to live and move in the kingdom of the Almighty.

› They wanted Jesus to assert Himself,

›› The Servant taught them that there is

and thus their own interests, confident that He would win the battle of the authorities.	authority in quietly turning a humiliating, deadly defeat into a lesson of victory.
› They didn't think one called "Lord" should wash feet.	›› The Servant reminded them that footwashing is what real ministry is all about.
› The disciples wanted to draw swords and fight to preserve their rights.	›› The Servant taught them by word and deed not to be so concerned with personal rights—but to turn the other cheek, go the second mile, and give to those who ask of you.
› They wanted to shrink away and hide, scared of their futures and their foes.	›› The Servant sent the Spirit that filled and enabled them to speak boldly before their enemies and preach His Word to all nations.

What the disciples wanted, and what they got, was not the same thing—at least initially. At the end of the process, however, the Servant had convinced them of the fallacy of their selfish wants, and the power of satisfied genuine needs. One of the most crucial roles of the servant teacher, then, is to offer the better, more Christlike, option to his students.

Second-Fiddle Teaching

Someone once asked Leonard Bernstein, the renowned conductor, what was the most difficult instrument to play. There was no problem answering that question. He responded, "Second fiddle. I can get plenty of first violinists, but to find one who plays second violin with as much enthusiasm or second French horn or second flute, now that's a problem. And yet if no one plays second, we have no harmony."[4]

The concept of "second fiddle" is what good teaching is all about. Drawing attention to ourselves is not the point, although a servant teacher may inadvertently do so. The goal is to play "second fiddle" to the "first chair"—the learner—for the kingdom promotion of our students and those they will eventually serve in turn. Ours is a supportive role, an attempt to help students live in harmony with their God and the problems and needs of their world. Self-fulfillment is not the key with the servant/teacher. Learner fulfillment is.

Jesus fulfills a "second fiddle" destiny. Obviously, the Godhead of which He is a part is the foundation of our faith. As a rabbi, it was His job to make sure His disciples knew that He was the Way, the Truth, and the Life—the "first fiddle." From a different perspective however, He seems to play the harmonious, supportive role of "second fiddle" as well. It was His intention that His associates be fulfilled and "do greater things" than even He was able to do on the earth. As we look back on His earthly didactic career, we are able to see this "second fiddle" aspect of His character and find ways to imitate it in our approaches to education. It means, in essence, that we examine our every approach to ensure that it allows people to stand upon our shoulders, so that they may be more than we could have been and do more than we could have done. That, and rejoicing when it happens, is the sign of teaching at its very best.

Beginning Steps . . .

1. *Be observant! When you notice one of your students in service—whether in class or through involvement in church, com-*

munity groups, volunteer organizations, scouting, etc.—applaud! Drop her a note, post newspaper clippings, "brag" about her to other people (including fellow students). Learn to speak positively about those nobody else seems to be talking much about.

2. *Adopt a class service project—serving a meal at the local soup kitchen, assisting elderly friends with yard work, conducting services at a prison—as an ongoing activity. Make priestly service a way of life for your group; reach out to others.*

3. *Divide a sheet of paper into two columns. On one side list what you perceive as your students' "wants," on the other side their "needs" as you see them. Which do you most often address in your teaching? Are there any interests common to both columns? Choose one of their needs to address in an upcoming lesson and find ways to serve them to meet that need.*

Jesus was not a theologian. He was God who told stories.

—Madeleine L'Engle

Therefore every one who hears these words of Mine and acts upon them may be compared to a wise man.

—Jesus

Jesus Would Have Us...

- ◗ Take the effect our words have very seriously,
- ◗ Use a wide repertoire of picturesque language,
- ◗ Develop a creative mix of stabilizing presuppositions and responsible manipulation of existing knowledge, held up to the light of the Holy Spirit.

CHAPTER NINE

HIS CREATIVE USE OF WORDS

Words are powerful!
"It seems the frailest of all weapons," said James Stalker in the 1891 Yale Lectures, "for what is a word? It is only a puff of air, a vibration trembling in the atmosphere for a moment and then disappearing . . . (Yet) though it be only a weapon of air, the word is stronger than the sword of the warrior."[1] As with the other principles presented in this volume, the teacher should pay special care to this aspect of communication. Words wed with wisdom can produce dividends for years to come. Slipshod communication inevitably produces slipshod results. Words are powerful! As teachers we must use them with exacting intent and a view toward creating a positive response. And lest we forget, the Teacher Himself was quick to remind us of the eternal results: "The mouth speaks out of that which fills the heart . . . I say to you, that every careless word that men shall speak, they shall render account for it in the day of judgment. For by your words you shall be justified, and by your words you shall be condemned" (Matt. 12:34b, 36, 37).

Aldous Huxley was wise to remind us that "words have power to mold men's thinking, to channel their feeling, to direct their willing and acting. Conduct and character are largely determined by the nature of the words we currently use to discuss ourselves and the world around us."[2] Jesus knew this. His words were carefully chosen to effect in His students the greatest change possible. His words were powerful because they emanated from the Source of Truth, proved themselves in experience, were consistent internally and with Jesus' actions, and were sent forth with redemptive purpose.

Aristotle developed the concept of "the golden mean." Simply stated, the golden mean held that all virtues represented the mean between two excesses. Commenting on this, William Barclay explains that "on the one hand there was the extreme of excess; on the other hand there was the extreme of defect; and in between there was the virtue itself, the happy medium."[3] When considering the role of words in teaching, I find this manner of arriving at the happy medium beneficial. At one extreme, words are everything, the most important aspect of education, the bedrock of pedagogy. At the other, they are worthless, the least of all educational elements, the most overused and overrated aspect of teaching. The question: How do we arrive at a proper synthesis?

I recall lying in bed one evening when I was in junior high, reading from *The Living Bible*. In the second chapter of Mark there appeared a few words that leapt from the page and struck me with such force that I have never forgotten them. "Talk is cheap," Jesus told the Jewish religious leaders after forgiving a paralyzed man on a stretcher; "anybody could say that. So I'll prove it to you by healing this man" (Mark 2:9-11, TLB) and He proceeds to back up His words with an act of physical cure. It should be noted that *The Living Bible* is not a direct translation. And as its preface recognizes, there are "dangers in paraphrases." But somehow, the "restatement of the original author's thoughts" at this point certainly did strike me that evening long ago as something that Jesus could well have said.

Those words have haunted me for years. "Talk is cheap." I have said that a hundred times in a number of situations and have always cast my vote with Ignatius, the early church Father, who wrote in A.D. 110 in his *Letter to the Romans* that "Christianity is not a matter of persuasive words."[4] But we know that, in fact, talk can be very powerful indeed. The faith of Jesus went far beyond talk. But never let it be denied that talk was a powerful tool, perhaps one of the most powerful tools, of the Teacher Jesus. The "golden mean" that we seek may simply be this: Talk can be cheap, but when it is backed up by action and experience, it is not only a powerful instrument of communication but potentially one of infinite value.

Are there limits to the educational value of words? Sure there are. Rev. David Preus, bishop emeritus of the former American Lutheran Church, reported recently that after 39 years of the ministry, "I have to say that our greatest public sin is that we are boring." Our lessons, he related, "are not so heretical as they are uninteresting."[5] Those are words that make us wince, but hopefully they also make us question whether we have done our best to make our words come alive. Testimony that is glibly delivered with no substantiation in the character and actions of the teacher effects little change. But if the teacher works to add a contemporary spice and practices a Jesus-style "teaching by walking around," then

The Kaleidoscope

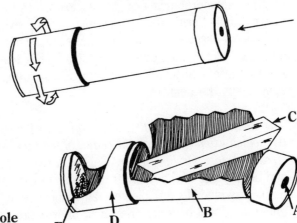

A—eyehole
B—funnel
C—reflector
D—manipulator
E—crystals

those words matched with redemptive activity and character have the power to transform.

Maximizing the Kaleidoscope

"The mind is like a kaleidoscope," a teacher told me some years back. To refresh my memory about that analogy, I recently made a jaunt to the toy store and bought one of those little contraptions that once mesmerized my youthful mind. It was as I remembered. You look in one end of the tube, you rotate the other end, and then you sit back to "oooh" and "aaah" over the beautiful configurations that appear through the eyehole.

Intrigued, I dissected the $1.47 scope to discover how these fascinating toys work. Unlike the brain, a kaleidoscope is an incredibly simple contraption. In other ways, however, some parallels between it and the mind might be drawn.

▲ *The tube (B) of the kaleidoscope holds a collection of vari-colored crystals.* This cylinder might represent the mind— that which contains the words, figures, images, and data gathered by the five senses. Jesus attempted to fill the conscious understanding of His disciples with a variety of information—Scripture, verbal instruction, events, and activities—essentially with a number of different-sized and vari-colored intellectual crystals. In His teaching He used a variety of words and experiences to impress lessons upon His hearers.

▲ *The images of the crystals bounce off a V-shaped reflector (C) which extends through the center of the tube, creating a circular image for the viewer.* This reflector brings order and beauty out of the many fragments. In the same way, Jesus provided His disciples certain principles by which to understand and organize their new information and experiences. These "givens" of the faith, to which He referred again and again in His words and actions, included the imperatives—to love both God and man, practice mercy, seek justice, and reflect the holiness of God.

164

They enabled the disciples to gain a more complete picture of truth.

▲ *By rotating the end (D) of the kaleidoscope, one can shift the colorful crystals into new configurations.* The teacher, and to some degree the learner, serve the same function. It is their job to manipulate the knowledge already acquired, shifting the growing collection of ideas and experiences to gain new insight and understanding. Jesus was a master of this process, and the disciples lent themselves to it, in varying degrees, by their availability and teachability. Jesus moved the disciples in new directions by telling unusual parables, speaking with unparalleled authority, and drawing comparisons with such profundity that His students undoubtedly wondered why they had never before noticed such truths in the everyday world.

▲ *The more crystals (E) placed in the kaleidoscope tube (including the widest variety of colors, shapes, and sizes) while still leaving room for movement, and the more they are manipulated, the greater and more beautiful the images created.* The Gospel of John declares that if all the things that Jesus said and did "were written in detail, I suppose that even the world itself would not contain the books which were written" (John 21:25). Jesus exposed His disciples to as much truth and as many experiences as they could absorb. Then He manipulated—in a very positive sense—these variegated ideas through the creative use of words and actions.

▲ *The kaleidoscope always works best and most vividly when held up to a light.* In fact, it won't work at all in a dark room and poorly in a dim room. It displays increasing effectiveness and beauty the greater light to which it is exposed. Likewise, Jesus continually challenged His disciples to expose their thoughts, words, and deeds to the Light of the Father—and with time—the Holy Spirit.

The kaleidoscope illustrates one way by which to view Jesus' didactic activity. He sought to provide His students new insights, different twists on old material, continued and effective manipulation of the combined ideas, and the opportunity and encouragement to always hold the working stuff of their new faith up to the light of the Godhead. New and creative synthesis—and it must be remembered that Jesus as Messiah was a new and creative synthesis for His Jewish world—can come only as the "kaleidoscope effect" is boldly utilized.

Roger Von Oech has written several books on creativity, one of which is entitled *A Whack on the Side of the Head*. In this fun-to-read volume he discusses this manipulation of the mind to move persons toward different syntheses. Von Oech says:

> *Knowledge is the stuff from which new ideas are made. Nonetheless, knowledge alone won't make a person creative. I think that we've all known people who knew lots of stuff and nothing creative happened. Their knowledge just sat in their crania because they didn't think about what they knew in any new ways. Thus, the key to being creative lies in what you do with your knowledge. Creative thinking requires an attitude or outlook which allows you to search for ideas and manipulate your knowledge and experience . . . Discovery consists of looking at the same thing as everyone else and thinking something different.*[6]

As teachers, we seek to effect creative, godly change in the lives of our students. But to accomplish this goal will require effective and creative use of words that will challenge our students to think and act with a godly difference.

The Picturesque Language of Jesus

The words of Jesus are, of necessity, a critical area of investigation for students of His teaching style. His words comprise nearly 20 percent of the entire New Testament; to study the Teacher we must study His words.

A kaleidoscope produces beautiful formations in part because of the varying size and colors of its many crystals. The job of the teacher is to provide or give the learner access to those crystals. Depending upon the audience, there are a number of ways to do this. Jesus related His lessons to the disciples and to the multitudes that gathered to hear Him speak. He knew that the vast majority of His audience, present and future, would be simple folk. To penetrate their reality, Jesus' words had to be simple yet challenging, touching on what they knew and bridging the way to what they needed to learn. I love the way Fred Craddock applies this dilemma to our modern situation: "The plain fact of the matter is that we are seeking to communicate with people whose experiences are concrete. . . . No farmer deals with the problem of calfhood, only with the calf. The woman in the kitchen is not occupied with the culinary arts in general but with a particular roast or cake. The wood craftsman is hardly able to discuss intelligently the topic of 'chairness,' but he is a master with a chair."[7]

It is true! Religious and educational professionals cannot reach the person on the street—our colleagues in the human experience—with the esoteric language often associated with theological minds. And that is as it should be. Theology, at its best, deals with the farmer as he pulls a young calf out of its mother's womb, or with the homemaker trying to figure out how to rake together thirty-four different ingredients for tonight's family dinner, or the carpenter wondering how to find meaning in building cabinets. Theology belongs in the home, in the marketplace, in the hospital, along the byways—essentially, everywhere God touches life. For teachers to overlook this dynamic in their contact with students is to miss the point of His intention.

An experiment conducted in 1979 demonstrates what Craddock has expressed. Participants in the study were asked to read, without further explanation, the following paragraph. Afterward they were asked to recall what they could from that single perusal:

The procedure is actually quite simple. First you arrange items into different groups. Of course one pile may be suffi-

cient depending on how much there is to do. If you have to go somewhere else due to lack of facilities that is the next step; otherwise, you are pretty well set. It is important not to overdo things. That is, it is better to do too few things at once than too many. In the short run this may not seem important but complications can easily arise. A mistake can be expensive as well. At first, the whole procedure will seem complicated. Soon, however, it will become just another facet of life. It is difficult to foresee any end to the necessity for this task in the immediate future, but then, one can never tell. After the procedure is completed one arranges the materials into different groups again. Then they can be put into their appropriate places. Eventually they will be used once more and the whole cycle will then have to be repeated. However, that is part of life.[8]

The above is simple language, but virtually meaningless without further explanation. The reader needs some kind of picture to make sense of the paragraph. One group was told in advance that this passage was about "washing clothes." (With that in mind, try re-reading the above sentences and see if your retention improves.) Another group read the paragraph much like you did the first time—without knowing what topic was being described. The question is: Which group comprehended the paragraph more effectively? Without being told of the "washing clothes" directive, the group who read the paragraph "cold" had a mean comprehension rating of 2.29 out of 7.00. Those who were given the "washing" picture had almost twice the score of their counterparts in the experiment—4.5 out of 7.00. Meaning is enhanced as people are able to "picture" our efforts at communication.

Jesus sought to deliver His message memorably, wrapped in language that His listeners could "see" and that connected with the lives of His hearers. Let's examine some of the techniques He utilized.

Parable: [*para* (beside) + *ballein* (to throw) . . . literally, to throw beside] A parable is a comparison that is "thrown beside" a truth to help clarify or accentuate a point. The parable may consist of a few short words—"Physician, heal yourself" (Luke 4:23)—or a full-blown story or allegory. The goal is to "drive home" a point by relating the abstract or propositional to something with which people can more readily identify. Parables and stories are easily remembered, which is no doubt why Jesus used so many of them. When describing the kingdom of heaven, for instance, He told many parables that brought the more familiar to bear light on the less familiar. In one chapter in the Gospel of Matthew Jesus sets forth six parables which begin with "the kingdom of heaven is like/may be compared to," similes which made a lasting impression on the people to whom He was speaking. The kingdom of heaven is like:

a man who sowed good seed in his field . . . (13:24 ff)
a mustard seed, which a man took and sowed . . . (13:31 ff)
leaven . . . (13:33 ff)
treasure hidden in a field . . . (13:44 ff)
a merchant seeking fine pearls . . . (13:45 ff)
a dragnet cast into a sea . . . (13:47 ff)

The shortest of these parables in Matthew 13 is 23 words—one sentence, one verse; the longest is 165 words—nine sentences, seven verses. Scripture contains parables both smaller and larger than these. Size matters little; what does matter is that, like Jesus, we learn to make use of the familiar to shed light upon the unfamiliar in a way that engages the learner in "crystal adding" activities. Jesus continued to add to His hearers' minds crystals of varying sizes, shapes, colors, and perspectives. Such teaching could not help but have a powerful effect on the disciples' future thinking. Also, notice how Jesus illuminates the "hard to understand" with the "easy to understand." In the kingdom parables He uses seeds, farmers, food ingredients, monetary value, a merchant, a familiar jewel, and the art of fishing. Each of these items was common to His Palestinian audience. You can imagine that with time, His disciples began forming a well-rounded and beautiful picture of the kingdom via the elements of the everyday.

THE MASTER PLAN OF TEACHING

Analogy: Analogies are comparisons between two or more elements. This technique is used brilliantly by Jesus in His speaking and teaching. Two of the most famous are the "You are the light of the world" (Matt. 5:14) and "You are the salt of the earth" (Matt. 5:13). With these analogies, Jesus pointed out to His listeners things that they knew by experience but may never have thought about in reference to their spiritual lives. Salt and light were concepts that communicated to the disciples.

Fresh analogies are always needed. They need to be biblically-based, with a contemporary message that makes listeners think and remember. One evangelist I know remarks that, since salt has been proven today to be detrimental to our health, the following variation might be apt: "You are the manure of the earth!" Stockpiled manure stinks, brings disease and insects, and is not in any way pleasant to have around. But farmers know that spread out manure fosters fertilization, growth, and new life. As teachers we must constantly keep our eyes open, as did Jesus, to the sights and sounds around us that point out and illumine scriptural truth.

Note some of the analogies that Jesus used: houses built on rock and sand, shepherds and sheep, yokes and burdens, birds, blind guides, employers and employees, bread, life, seeds, plants, coins, water, masters and servants, vineyards, vines and branches. He also employed the technique of contrast, differentiating between builders and virgins, sheep and goats, light and darkness, rich and poor, and younger and older. These examples provided vivid pictures from the everyday life of those to whom He spoke. All were fodder for eternal insight.

Parables and analogies attempt the communication of truth through word pictures. An Arabian proverb notes that "he is the best teacher who can turn the ear into an eye"—who uses picturesque language, or words that people can see.

Dialogue: There is something very special about dialogue. As one writer noted, you should not send your "teaching mail" to "Occupant" or "Current Resident." Personalize, personalize,

personalize! That is the strength of open and free-flowing discussion. Truth, instead of soaring over our heads, has a unique potential to speak directly to the one addressed. Some assert that very little real dialogue is apparent in the teaching of Jesus. I disagree. Scripture records, for instance, over 150 questions used by Jesus at various points of His ministry. He might well have agreed with the sentiment expressed by Machiavelli: "A prince should be a great asker of questions."[9] And while it was the primary intent of the Gospel writers to record Jesus' words rather than the comments of others, we certainly might extrapolate from the evidence that there was much interchange at work. Also, Jesus frequently supped with friends and acquaintances at their homes and other gatherings. Might we not assume that there was a great deal of dialogue in those times of informal give and take?

When the disciples returned from their preaching mission Jesus withdrew with them to receive a report on their ministry. Jesus then invited them to a lonely place to rest a while, undoubtedly for a time of dialogue and instruction based on their experiences (Mark 6:30, Luke 9:10). Could it be that such dialogue was an ongoing process? Can you imagine the disciples with Jesus in a boat on the Sea of Galilee chatting, arguing back and forth, and questioning each other as they made their way across the water? Can't you imagine them enroute to the next town, clustered in small groups and immersed in conversation? Dialogue was the rule of the rabbinic mode of teaching. Jesus, it would appear both implicitly and explicitly, exercised this technique frequently in travels and journeys with His disciples.

Contemporary education could use a resurgence of dialogue. James Garfield once noted, "I am not willing that this discussion should close without mention of the value of a true teacher. Give me a log hut, with only a simple bench, Mark Hopkins [president of Williams College] on one end and I on the other, and you may have all the buildings, apparatus, and libraries without him."[10] The teacher in hot pursuit of the Jesus style of education will take note: dialogue teaches.

Situation: Perhaps the most powerful of Jesus' words came

naturally out of situations which He encountered. Take, for instance, the words of Jesus recorded in John 11. The setting is the grave of Lazarus at Bethany. The words are those of Martha and Jesus:

Martha: *"Lord, if You had been here, my brother would not have died."*

Jesus: *"I am the resurrection and the life; he who believes in Me shall live even if he dies, and everyone who lives and believes in Me shall never die. Do you believe this?"*

Martha: *"I know that he will rise again in the resurrection on the last day."*

Jesus: *"Remove the stone."*

Martha: *"Lord, by this time there will be a stench, for he has been dead four days."*

Jesus: *"Did I not say to you, if you believe, you will see the glory of God? Lazarus, come forth!"*

Those words are powerful. In the life of Jesus they grew out of need, a dramatic, sad situation, and an unparalleled opportunity for His disciples and all others present to watch Jesus interact with the sisters, weep, verbalize a powerful lesson or two, and then raise a friend from the dead.

Consider another situation. A young man ran up to Jesus while He was setting out on a journey. "Teacher, what good thing shall I do that I may obtain eternal life?" Jesus responded, "Keep the commandments." "All these things I have kept," said the young man. "If you wish to be complete, go and sell your possessions and give to the poor . . . and follow Me." After the man walked away sadly, "for he was one who owned much property," Jesus made a remarkable comment to the disciples, "It is hard for a rich man to enter the kingdom of heaven . . . it is easier for a camel to go through the eye of a needle than for a rich man to enter the kingdom of God." The disciples, astonished, asked who in the world could be saved. Their Jewish background had always taught that the rich were privileged and favored by God. Jesus told them, "With men this is impossible, but with God all things are possible" (Matt. 19:16-26).

The disciples remembered those words because they had grown out of a picture in the making; they had arisen out of an actual situation. That situation and those words suggested several things to the inner circle of Jesus' students: (1) not everyone that wants to be involved can be, (2) wealth can be deadly to kingdom causes, (3) their Jewish tradition might not be as on target as they had been led to believe, and (4) men and their might cannot save, only God can.

Undoubtedly, the above discussion does not exhaust the possibilities associated with Jesus' use of words. There is no limit to the number of "crystals" that can be placed in the mind of the student. Some people, after spending years of ministry in a particular locale, eagerly request a move, shouting as they go, "I'm spent! I've said all I have to say here!" That is possible, but the teacher who looks through Jesus' eyes is capable of seeing infinite possibilities for communication. Jesus drew upon a variety of methods, pictures, and resources to sound His message clearly. Words interwoven with moving experiences were a vital part of Jesus' teaching style. They should be a part of ours as well.

I'll never forget an experience recounted by my college professor. During his undergraduate years, this man's favorite professor held up a pen and issued a challenge to this would-be teacher: if he could say everything there was to say about the simple instrument, the professor would grant his pupil $10,000. "Make a list," he said, "and I will look at it and say several more things about that writing utensil that you have not even thought of." My teacher took him up on the challenge. He made a list of 300 observations. He spent the better part of a day thinking of "just one more thing" he could say about the pen. Finally, he proudly strode into the professor's office, presented the pen and the list and then listened as the professor named ten things—for starters—that the young man had not written down. As my teacher related this story to us in class he said, "You can't exhaust the possibilities. New perspectives are endless." In short, we should never run out of things to teach. There is always another perspective, another idea, or another "crystal."

The Words of Jesus . . . A Compact Example

I am indebted to Ralph Lewis, friend and professor at Asbury Theological Seminary, for the following outline and analysis of Jesus' Sermon on the Mount.[11] Here we find a clear description of Jesus' playful, illustrative, and highly entertaining use of words:

I. Analogies—5:3-16
Poor, mourners, meek, merciful, pure, peacemakers, persecuted, salt, light.

II. Attitudes—5:17-48
Self-righteousness, hate, lust, respect, honesty, revenge, love, giving, prayer, fasting, greed, anxiety, judging, faith, choice.

III. Actions—6:1–7:23
Give, pray, fast, work, serve, don't worry.

IV. Alternatives—7:24-29
Gates, fruits, trees, foundations.

Words	2,320
Images, pictures, examples, illustrations (wolves, sheep, fruit, light, rock, sand, storm, build, etc.)	348 or 1/7th
Comparisons	142 or 1/16th
Verbs for energy/action	404 or 1/6th
Present tense/relevance, realism	65% approximately
Future tense	30% approximately
Past tense	5% approximately
Varied viewpoints	42 different aspects of happiness
Questions	Asks nineteen questions giving it an overall feel of dialogue and involvement on the part of the learner.

In short, says Lewis, this teaching event is "chock-full of analogies and references to experience the people could easily relate to."[12] Further, Jesus here "and in other teachings, begins with the known, the concrete, the personal to guide hearers to the unknown, the abstract, and the universal."[13] Lewis points out that the Master repeatedly returns to familiar and concrete terms for conveying abstract concepts: forty-nine times He refers to sheep, twenty-seven times to sowing, twenty-two times to reaping and harvesting, and ten times to water imagery. The job of the educator, as Jesus demonstrates in this sermon, is to seize upon such obvious points of contact with the Creator and utilize them to communicate truth. Parables, analogies, questions, and dialogue—like kaleidoscope crystals—create a vivid picture of the Good News.

The opening paragraphs of this chapter mentioned other elements, from the analogy of the kaleidoscope, crucial to the creative use of words. Dissect a kaleidoscope from any toy store and find the V-shaped insert which reflects the crystals into beautiful images. It is an immovable constant within the tube. Extracted to Jesus' teaching style the reflector represents the absolutes of the faith, those organizing principles which give meaning to the ideas and experiences which we assimilate:

▲ The holiness of God
▲ The inspiration and authority of His Word
▲ The purpose and fallenness of man
▲ The means of redemption of man through Jesus Christ

It is the teacher's job to present and reiterate these principles, providing students a framework within which to organize the crystals continually being gathered through word and activity. At every point of the educational endeavor they should be repeated—creatively and with variety—to maintain focus and balance.

Keith Tonkel, with whom I work, is one of the best I know at this teaching task. With an inner-city ministry like his, it is important to constantly remind parishioners of the church's reason for existing in the place and the manner in which it does. In other words, why doesn't the church move to a more prominent location in the community? Tonkel takes every opportunity to creatively address this question of purpose—during sermons, in the Sunday morning announcement period, in conversations, etc. A recent bulletin of Wells United Methodist Church contained the following reminder:

WHY NOT MOVE INTO A DECENT NEIGHBOR-HOOD? We've had that question asked, and often. The answer is that first: We believe this to be a neighborhood of decent people. And secondly: We know that when the physical environment changes, many groups feel that they should move too. Our feeling and the leadership of God was that we should stay. For us it is the right rather than expedient thing to do. We remain open to God's direction as we understand it. But this is where we are to serve just now. Thanks for being part of that understanding.

Over and over, week after week, Tonkel presses home such teaching on the "Wells Incarnation." He speaks to other constants for the Wellsfolk as well: Jesus, the church, communion, the Apostle's Creed, "free worship," and "why we do things the way we do." The point is, Tonkel has recognized an important concept: People need to understand the groundwork for their existence and behavior, as individuals and as a corporate church body. When they do, then the crystals of pastoral teaching and corporate experience can bounce off of this inner stabilizer, creating a design with meaning, order, and beauty.

I also mentioned that manipulation of the crystals is necessary to produce ever-changing blends of color. In today's world, the word manipulation often carries negative connotations, but according to the dictionary it simply means to "work, alter, or handle skillfully." That process is essential if the varying viewpoints and perspectives are to be brought together in meaningful synthesis. Such manipulation can come in the form of words or experiences that challenge the mind of the student to think in new ways.

I have observed evangelist Ravi Zacharias achieve this effect with consummate skill. Zacharias is able to weave an intricate web of confusion that is fascinating to hear but often leaves the audience wondering in midstream, "Where in the world is he going with what he is talking about?" One evening several friends and I attended a service where Zacharias was speaking. Young preacher-boys ourselves, we were spellbound and confused. "Where is he going with all this?" one of my buddies whispered. All I could do was shrug my shoulders. About five minutes later, with one awesome sentence, he pulled together three major crystals: illustrations about Mother Teresa, Adolph Hitler, and Bertrand Russell. It happened so suddenly and with such force that my friends and I were wide-eyed for several moments before we all stood up and cheered wildly. Well, actually, we cheered an hour later back at the dormitory. But manipulation "Ravi Zacharias style" was exciting. With one well-placed verbal entry he turned our minds in a new direction and provided a learning experience that we still remember.

The ultimate in such manipulation doesn't come through mere words, however. For the Twelve, it happened in the coming of the Holy Spirit. Suddenly, with the redemptive presence of that Person, all the disciples' training took on new meaning and sharpened focus. The coming and death of Jesus made sense. Words that once confused now exploded with meaning and insight. From that point they would never act, think, or speak the same. The effectual manipulation of the crystals which Jesus had carefully cultivated changed the course of the world.

And, lest we forget, the kaleidoscope of the mind always works best when held up to the Light. The Illuminator is eager to fulfill His role, but we must hold our teaching up to Him to discover the impact of His Light upon our instruction and, ultimately, our lives.

Playful Learning
Benjamin Bloom, one of the foremost educational researchers of our generation, has concluded that people who exhibit ex-

ceptional talent in a given field were usually introduced to that field of endeavor in a playful manner. He comments upon Alfred North Whitehead and the *Aims of Education:* "Whitehead believed that there are rhythms of learning. For example, no matter at what age you start learning science, you should begin to learn it playfully, almost romantically, with wonderful teachers who make it exciting and interesting."[14]

This "playful" introduction to the subject is followed later by more precise instruction as to underlying principles and the development of accuracy and skill. But the foundation is laid in the initial approach of playfulness. Roger Von Oech writes that the ancient Greek concept for education (*paideia*) is almost identical to their concept for play (*paidia*). They knew, he suggests, that "learning comes from playing." Von Oech comments: "Perhaps Plato was thinking this when he said, 'What, then, is the right way of living? Life must be lived as play.' If you are playing, then you are still learning and living."[15]

Jesus' approach to education was much in the mode of this kind of playful activity. He attended parties, jaunted around the countryside preaching and praying, found joy in interpersonal relations, and interacted meaningfully with His environment. It is no surprise that His words were reflective of such play. He spoke picturesquely about people, events, nature, and the kingdom here and in the future. He spoke both humorously and harshly, softly and loudly. As with all play, there were times of relaxed enjoyment and times of increased intensity, but always with a goal in mind. The goal of Jesus seemed to be to pound home His message of holiness within a learning atmosphere that led His disciples from one level of growth to the next.

Elton Trueblood reminds us, "Once we realize that Christ was not always engaged in pious talk, we have made an enormous step on the road to understanding." He adds that, to our loss, "Religion, we think, is serious business, and serious business is incompatible with banter."[16] The fact is that we have often developed a false pattern of Christ's character. Though we do not always say so directly, we habitually think of Him as mild in manner, endlessly patient, grave in speech, and serious almost to the point of dourness. We try to explain away any words or incidents in the Gospels which are inconsistent with such a picture. But if we abandon this effort and "sit down before the facts as a little child," with a minimum of presupposition, we come out with a radically different conception.[12]

Learning with Jesus in the Gospels reads like playful adventure story. It was not mere frivolity, but the kind of engaging and spontaneous education that led the disciples, in good time, toward a profound spiritual maturity. Accuracy and skill with the principles and specifics of the faith would come soon enough; better to let them wait than to stunt growth by providing babes with verbal nutrition that they were not yet able to digest.

Trueblood writes: "Van Doren noted that the supremacy of Shakespeare lay not in that 'he saw what nobody ever saw before.' Not true. Instead, 'he saw what everyone has seen, but with a clarity, an intensity, and finally a humility which makes his subject even more interesting to us than he is.' "[18] What Trueblood related about Shakespeare is undoubtedly true of Jesus. Seeing the deep realities of God with clarity, intensity, and humility and communicating them with words that reflect those qualities was the pattern and challenge of "the master plan of teaching."

Beginning Steps . . .

1. *Scan newspapers and magazines in search of relevant illustrations. Books, TV, movies, song lyrics — all media are potential sources. What do you find that would grab the attention of your students and aid the retention of biblical truth?*

2. *Keep a file of illustrations, ideas, and quotes on note cards. Develop a filing system that allows you to put your hand on any card you want within two minutes.*

3. *Evaluate your teaching to determine if you are communicating what you intend. (Is your message helped or hindered by your*

inflection, speed, body language, facial expressions, etc? Could you be boring people? Are you relevant, applying biblical truths to life situations?

Audio and video equipment, where available, are helpful for self-evaluation.

Provide a self-test at the end of each lesson to see if students have caught your main point(s).

Ask a colleague to observe and critique your teaching method. Pass out evaluation forms to class members.

When the results from these evaluations are in, target one or two areas for improvement.

Concerning Him . . . the testimony is given that He had
twelve disciples through whom His wonderful word of
salvation was to be accomplished. These same
twelve disciples went out in the known part
of the world and proclaimed His majesty
with lovingkindness and serious intent.
—Aristides, philosopher, A.D. 137

Go therefore and make disciples of
all nations, baptizing them . . . and . . .
teaching them to do all things I have commanded.
—Jesus

The Master's Plan Calls for . . .

▶ Reproducing disciples in His image,
▶ Recognizing and avoiding the dangers
   that would deter us in our calling,
▶ Enabling disciples to live the whole
   Gospel,
▶ Committing our lives to instilling the
   Gospel into the lives of men, women,
   boys, and girls.

CHAPTER TEN

REPRODUCING THE VISION

Les Spencer approached Dawson Trotman about one of his shipmates. Trotman, one day to be famous the world over for founding The Navigators, had spent hours with Spencer in Bible study, and inculcating key spiritual disciplines. Spencer was excited about the progress he was making and wanted his friend and fellow sailor Gurney Harris to visit the Trotman home and get in on some of the excitement.

"Daws, I'd sure like to get Gurney over here to learn what you're teaching me," he once remarked.

"Sure he can come," was the answer. "But why don't you get him started? Just pass on to him what I'm giving you."

"I haven't had the training," Les objected.

"Doesn't matter," Dawson looked him in the eye. "If you can't teach him what I've taught you, I've failed."[1]

The greatness of a teacher is not measured by how impressed people are with a presentation or by their delight in a personality. The true greatness of a teacher lies in how the values and character he or she seeks to communicate are passed on—reproduced—in succeeding generations. Betty Lee Skinner, in her biography of Trotman, pens the following entry: "It was Dawson's growing conviction that more could be accomplished for God by building in depth in one life than by scattering shot in all directions, ministering to groups only once or occasionally. He had copied a quotation in his Bible: 'Emotion is no substitute for action.' He now added, 'Action is no substitute for production.'[2]

Trotman was a great teacher. And like all educators of distinction, he knew that production, and reproduction, was the key to a vital movement. As he would readily attest, he was simply following the mode of the Master.

Jesus the Reproducer

In retrospect it is rather easy to recognize the pattern Jesus established. He surrounded Himself with a few intense learners, trained them, and then unleashed this educated corps to emulate their Master's disciple-making process around the world. The entire package of the Gospels and the Acts of the Apostles substantiates this pattern. Perhaps nowhere is it more emphasized, however, than in the final words of Jesus in Matthew's Gospel: "Go, therefore, and make disciples of all nations, baptizing them in the name of the Father and of the Son and of the Holy Spirit, teaching them to do all things I have commanded you" (Matt. 28:19-20).

By examining the Greek text we can discover some valuable points that don't come across in our English versions of these verses:

1. Three of the words in these verses are participles. They serve to supplement the main verb and are dependent on it. First is *poreuthentes,* translated "go" in most versions but more accurately rendered "going." Second is *baptizontes,* or "baptizing." Third is *didaskontes* or "teaching." In addition, tense indicates that "going" carried imperative force or is a command, and "baptizing" and "teaching" are to be continuous and ongoing activities.
2. There is one main verb which constitutes the thrust of the message in these verses and which the participles complement. That verb is *matheteusate,* which means "make disciples," and it is the heart of the Commission. The Twelve were to go, teach, baptize, to be sure, but all to the end of making disciples. Presumably this was in imitation of their

own experience with Jesus. *Make disciples* is the main message in this passage.

THE GREAT COMMISSION

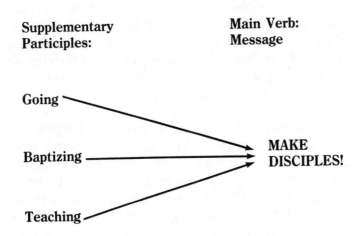

Supplementary Participles:

Going

Baptizing

Teaching

Main Verb: Message

MAKE DISCIPLES!

In the final moments of His ministry to the disciples, Jesus commissioned them to repeat in the lives of others the process He had just completed in theirs. The disciples, if taking Him in strict literal fashion, would have each moved out in the world and found exactly twelve disciples in whom to invest their lives. While that could have happened without our knowing it (since we have little detail in Scripture about most of the apostles), it is more likely that they took the principles of Jesus' teaching and methodology and applied them in future ministry. If so, we may suppose that:

▲ Each sought to become "incarnate" within the culture in which he ministered—identifying, learning, embodying, targeting, relating, and taking the necessary time to make disciples.
▲ They propagated small groups of believers intent on love, accountability, and care for one another.
▲ These small groups were marked by redemptive action in

their communities as they witnessed human needs and moved quickly to meet them.

▲ The disciples moved out to serve like their Master, not be served in the fashion of earthly royalty.

▲ The implications of the Jesus model impacted the totality of the disciples' lives: their families, their churches, their support of the kingdom at large.

▲ The converts to the Christ movement went to great effort — even death — to remain faithful to their cause, and to introduce others to their Saviour and build them up in mature faith.

That Jesus expected such a response on the disciples' part is not surprising. John James Vincent reminds us that when the disciples were beckoned to "follow Me" it was constantly implied, as well as expressed, that they were to "become a living embodiment of the same way, to copy the same actions, to speak the same message in word and deed, to become an 'acted parable' of the same kingdom, to share the same fate, to assimilate the doctrine of the Master."[3] That was the underlying and implicit duty of a disciple in the Palestine of their day. They were called to embody the message themselves, and prepare to perpetuate it.

I have always enjoyed the inspiring challenge to commitment contained in C.S. Lewis' writings. One of the most intriguing is his description of Christianity in the modern day classic, *Mere Christianity*. He writes "Enemy-occupied territory, that is what the world is. Christianity is the story of how the rightful king has landed, you might say landed in disguise, and is calling us all to take part in a great campaign of sabotage."[4] I like those two sentences. The rightful King has landed, all right — as an itinerant rabbi. Over the period of a few years, this teacher challenged a handful of common men to take over the world for the kingdom of God. The "campaign of sabotage" is evident in Christ's instruction to His disciples to go forth and be the kind of teachers and disciple makers they were capable of being by the grace of God. They were beckoned to flip the world right-side up again.

Neil Postman and Charles Weingartner once wrote a book entitled *Teaching as a Subversive Activity*. I sense that might well be the perspective of the Gospels in describing the activity of Jesus. Here comes God in the flesh, living and breathing a revolutionary message of love and strongly recommending that His closest associates spread the revolution across the land. Subversive? You bet. The undercover agents? Teachers inspired by and emulating the greatest educator of them all.

Dangers to Avoid
The call to reproduce was clearly sounded by Jesus. For any budding movement, however, dangers and deterrents abound. This was true for the believers who catapulted out of Galilee to the ends of the earth to spread the message of Jesus. It will be no different for us. Unfortunately the gravest dangers are more insidious than we might expect.

Danger #1: Complacency via Organization
Sociologists often differentiate between sects and ecclesiae. Sect is the terminology used to designate a relatively new, less formally organized religious organization. An example of a sect would be the early Christian movement, for instance, although it should be noted that all religious movements basically begin at this stage of development. In contrast to this paradigm is what sociologists terms the ecclesia—sociological jargon for stable and institutionalized religious organizations. The key to understanding the development of religious groups is that sects tend to gradually become institutionalized and turn into ecclesiae. If you look at any major denomination, you can usually identify the pattern.

Sects, for instance, have a rather loose organizational structure; few or no officials; the religious duties fall upon the shoulders of the members who exhibit a high degree of involvement; members tend to be on the lower end of the occupational spectrum; labor diligently for converts to their frame of reference and eagerly encourage others to join their movement; display a vital concern over the depth and purity of their standards; and frequently have a radical set of beliefs, and oppose, even unto death, compromising their ideals.

Ecclesiae, on the other hand, are stable and institutionalized with many officials; accept administrative and clerical hierarchies with professionals doing much of the movement's work; are made up of middle to upper class members who are well established in their communities; focus much energy inward so that there is less concern with converts; demonstrate less concern for depth and purity of doctrinal stances; adopt many secular standards from the cultural status quo and have a broad-based attitude of compromise if their religious beliefs contradict the cultural norm.

Sociologists conclude that it is difficult to differentiate between contemporary sectarian and ecclesiastical movements because sects gradually become like the institutions against which they once reacted. Also, it is possible for sects to exist within the framework of an ecclesiastical structure. Often, however, they have a difficult time doing so (e.g., the first-century Church within Judaism) and are forced through circumstances to become distinct groupings.

Sociologists present these paradigms to help us understand the development of religious organizations, but elements of both sect and ecclesia are likely needed within any healthy church movement. For instance, an active, productive denomination needs both vital lay participation and wise, strong leadership with responsible training to provide stability. But here is the danger: Reproduction and the cultivation of Christlike disciples are far more likely within groups that exhibit strong sectarian elements. In most cases, they do not occur as naturally within the more formalized and well-established structure of the ecclesia. The retention of sectarian elements is imperative if the educational methodology of Jesus is to be emulated with any kind of accuracy.

In essence, the move toward the ecclesia is dangerous, for it saps energy from a frame of reference whose primary concern was to get its message—at all costs—out to those who do not yet know.

Think of it: Like a sectarian, Jesus modeled a method marked by the participation of all members. Although a hierarchy existed, it was one of self-denying service, not of one–upmanship. Active involvement was expected, as was a growing sense of purity and depth. Money was a tool for ministry, not for prestige or gain. Evangelization of the poor and service to the downtrodden was the norm. After Pentecost a high degree of commitment was evident, even unto death. Lackadaisical dependence upon professionals and organized bureaucracy was nil. The tenets of those early believers were definitely contrary to mainstream Jewish thought. In short, Jesus and His disciples seem in many respects to be a sect with a revolutionary call to reproduce.

Once these sectarian elements are mitigated and the movement begins to resemble the extreme forms of the ecclesia, however, the educational model of Jesus fades into the background. At this point a revived church educational model, rediscovering the primitive elements needed for effective instruction, must be developed within the established ecclesia.

A few years ago I spoke at a retreat for the bishops and executives of my denomination. I was relatively young at the time and therefore extremely cautious in my presentations. I anticipated a future with this group and the denomination they served and was sure that saying something controversial would immediately snuff out my chances. At one of the evening meetings, however, I decided to risk the following illustration created by John M. Dresher:

Now it came to pass that a group existed which called themselves fisherman. And lo, there were many fish in the water all around. In fact, the whole area was surrounded by streams and lakes filled with fish. And they were hungry.

Week after week, month after month, and year after year, these who called themselves fishermen met in meetings and talked about their call to fish, the abundance of fish and how they might go about fishing. Year after year they carefully defined what fishing means, defended fishing as an occupation and declared that fishing is always to be a primary task of fisherman.

And so . . .
—They developed nifty slogans.
—They built an elaborate, beautiful set of buildings called "Fishing Headquarters."
—They organized a board to send out fishermen to other places where there were many fish of different colors, and challenged each other to be true to their call to fishing.
—The board hired staffs, appointed committees, and held many meetings in order to define fishing, defend fishing and decide what new streams should be explored.
—Training centers were built in order to teach fisherman how to fish, offering courses on the needs of fish, the nature of fish, where to locate fish, psychological reactions of fish, and how to approach and feed fish. The teachers had doctorates in fishology. But they didn't fish; they only taught fishing.
—They sponsored costly national—even worldwide—congresses to discuss fishing, ways of fishing, show off new fishing equipment, and introduce novel invitations to fishermen and new kinds of bait.
—Publishing houses produced interesting fishing guides. Presses printed materials devoted to the crying need for new methods, better equipment, and insightful programs.

After one stirring meeting on 'The Necessity for Fishing,' one young fellow left the meeting and went fishing. The next day he reported he had caught two outstanding fish. He was honored for his excellent catch and scheduled to visit all the big meetings possible to tell how he did it. So he quit his fishing in order to have time to tell about the experience to the other fishermen. He was also placed on the Fishermen's General Board as a person having considerable experience. . . .

Imagine how hurt some were when one day a person suggested that those who didn't catch fish were really not fishermen, no matter how much they claimed to be. Yet it did sound correct. Is a person a fisherman if year after year he never catches a fish? Is one following if he isn't fishing?[25]

I ended the illustration with, Jesus said, "Follow Me, and I will make you fishers of men" (Matt. 4:19).

The denominational executives took it all in good fun. Several times I was interrupted by laughter, but also by nods of understanding. One of the bishops approached me soon after the talk and asked for a copy of the illustration. He saw in those few paragraphs the subtle danger and temptation for the Church to become an overdeveloped "ecclesia" capable of reproducing only its own bureaucracy. The bishop recognized what we all know in our hearts. If we are not careful, instead of making disciples, we are apt to just create another committee. Instead of producing a living organism we are liable to spawn just another nonproductive organization. Instead of a movement empowered by the life of Jesus, we are likely to be characterized by polite audiences listening to religious platitude delivered by polished professionals. As those interested in perpetuating Jesus' methods and message, we should be on guard against an "ecclesiastical" form of bondage that threatens to assail from within our collective bodies. The disciple intent on reproduction will recognize this tendency and seek a way to call students back to the primitive message and method of Jesus.

Danger #2: Underestimating the Power of Multiplication
The parable is well-known but bears repeating. A soldier had performed heroically in war and was, because of his courageous acts, invited to a private audience with the king. The king, overjoyed that the empire had been saved, offered the hero whatever his heart desired—up to half of his vast domain. The wise champion, prepared for just such a moment, laid a small mat at the king's feet. The mat was divided into sixty-four squares and his request was simple.

"Grant me," the defender humbly proposed, "one grain on the first of these squares. Double the grain from one square to the next for each square (one then two then four then eight then sixteen, etc.) until your Majesty has complete the number of squares on this small mat." The king was stunned. "That is all you desire?" he queried with a smile. "That is all," affirmed the shrewd soldier.

191

That is enough! Try it yourself. If you figure correctly you will go over 1 million grains at the twenty-first square. Before the final square of that mat is smothered, the kingdom, regardless of its size, will be several feet under seed. Somewhere down the line, the king will undoubtedly have lost both his grin and his temper. And the hero will be a rich man if he can find a way to transform the grain of the kingdom into profit. Such is the power of multiplication.

For the sake of argument, let's suppose the hero of our story had requested a flat thousand grains per square. At the end he would have had a nice little pile, but unless there was famine in the kingdom he wouldn't have been a wealthy man. In the same light, multiplication as the mandate to make disciples in the teaching style of Jesus has humble beginnings. It does not seem impressive at first; initially, it may not strike us as being a wise expenditure of time. But if the students of this method are faithful and continue to reach out and reproduce, the impact is impressive. We can preach exclusively if we desire, but at best that model will produce only a ministry of addition. Small group discipleship as modeled by Jesus is the wisest expenditure of our time over the long run.

One teacher, with whom I discussed the multiplication principle, was frustrated because he felt a need to reach the people of India with the Gospel. Why the frustration? He had no means to get there, no definite call of God to go, and a situation at home that prevailed upon him to stay put. Then one day a young student, eager to learn from and be mentored by this teacher, enrolled at the school where he taught. As a result, the mission was fulfilled and in a way far better than the teacher had envisioned. Through an intense interpersonal relationship the professor and his wife discipled the student and his spouse. Today they are planting churches among Hindus in the rural regions of India.

I interviewed another teacher who employs a similar method in his ministry and asked if it had had any substantial impact. "It has had small success," he began humbly. "Because of this discipleship effort over the past few years, we have people reproducing themselves in Monterrey, Mexico; Medellín, Colombia; Londrina, Brazil; Madrid, Spain; and in areas scattered throughout France, Zaire, and Taiwan." Grabbing a quick breath, he went on to add, "We also, obviously, have people across America working with folks in small groups and making disciplemakers." He paused before concluding with a decided understatement. "So, while it isn't very impressive yet, we're still working on it."

Here is one teacher multiplying himself, literally, around the world. I can attest that there are folks in corners of the country and world who will point back to that disciplemaker as instrumental in their lives and callings. Does the method work? To those who have effectively implemented the teaching style of Jesus that is almost a silly question.

Reproducers who get less press but whose results are just as impressive are those involved in Sunday School classes and home Bible study groups scattered across the country. Challenged by teachers yoked with Jesus, saints around the world extend redemptive activity to factories, small businesses, schools, and other spheres of influence, forming their own small groups bent on producing reproducers. It is no wonder that many of today's most effective pastors, teachers, and church leaders, in response to the question, "What influence in your Christian pilgrimage most profoundly affected your life?" commonly reply, "The Christian small group" or "The teacher that took the time to invest in my life."

Benjamin Bloom, suggesting key criteria for master-teachers, named the production of "demonstrable results" as foundational. The teacher who understands the power of the reproduced message and method of Jesus coupled with a respect for the power of multiplication will fulfill one of the most fundamental keys for earning the title "master."[6]

Danger #3: Lack of Wholistic Reproduction
Jesus taught the whole person for the whole world. While His educational contemporaries were frequently less than wholistic in their approach and teaching, Jesus was faithful to impress upon His students the well-rounded emphases of His kingdom vision.

One of the dangers of reproduction is that the disciple may be something quite apart from what Jesus had planned. As a sectarian movement evolves, for instance, the gravest risk is that the second generation will differ just slightly in their fundamental presuppositions, the third generation will then change a bit more, and soon the movement is a far cry from where it initially began. Disciples intent on reproducing Christlikeness had better first understand what is to be produced. The question needs to be asked: What constitutes wholistic Christian living? What did Jesus intend for His disciples? It is an important consideration, for errors in our presuppositions can mean disaster when those errors come to fruition. To omit any element of Jesus' approach is error. We should strive intentionally therefore to be wholistic in our presentation of Christian discipleship.

Wholistic Discipleship

Jesus seems to be in agreement with the rabbis of His day on one crucial point: Ignorance on theological or scriptural issues was no virtue. As do all teachers, Jesus desired that His students possess a base of knowledge to guide their future activity. He was masterfully adept at putting truths in a nutshell, giving His disciples "hooks" on which they could hang the rest of their thought and mission. Devout Jews of Jesus' day had well over 600 laws and regulations which they sought to learn and obey. Yet when a Pharisee once asked Jesus, "Teacher, which is the great commandment in the Law?" His answer was both brief and comprehensive, consisting of two essentially inseparable elements: (1) Love God, and (2) Love man, and do both wholeheartedly (Matt. 22:35 ff). As the Rabbi Akiba once remarked about a lesson, after these commandments "all the rest is commentary." But Jesus did not stop there. He exposed and illustrated these laws with Old Testament Scriptures and with stories, maxims, epigrams, questions, conversations, discourses, and demonstrations during the course of their travels. After three years of such experiences, Jesus had undoubtedly impacted the disciples' thinking, their capacity for insightful analysis, their power of reasoning, and their ability to form truthful opinions. The apostles would need such skills when out among the heathen societies where their beliefs would be challenged and mocked. Without a "Christian mind" and the capacity to withstand the intellectual challenges, they would have crumbled at the hands of a world disinterested in another mindless religion.

Some will undoubtedly object, *"But I'm no theologian"* — implying that they are not, and quite frankly that they don't want to be. But theology (literally, *theos*, God, + *logos*, idea/thought/saying) means god-thoughts, sayings, or ideas. Everyone thinks, has ideas, or talks about God. Therefore, in essence, everyone is a theologian. Our task is to be sure we think rightly and to *help others think rightly* about Him and His purposes for the world. That is one of the tasks of Christian education.

However, our task goes much further than cognitive stimulation. John Wesley went so far as to suggest that right opinion was but a slender part of religion, if it could be allowed to be any part of it at all. Wesley believed:

> *Whatsoever the generality of people may think, it is certain that opinion is not religion: No, not right opinion; assent to one, or to ten thousand truths. There is a wide difference between them: Even right opinion is as distant from religion as the east is from the west. Persons may be quite right in their opinions, and yet have no religion at all; and, on the other hand, persons may be truly religious, who hold many wrong opinions.* [7]

Wesley did not mean to denigrate the intellectual life. But it could not then, and cannot today, stand alone. Our second emphasis in a wholistic model of education is to cultivate *the inner life of devotion.* The typical layperson (and the clergy, too!) today prays, on the average, a couple of minutes daily. Many professed Christians do not even pray and read the Scripture at all outside of what might occur on Sunday mornings. This should be a cause of deep concern for educators. Certainly it is contrary to our Lord's model, for by His own consistent example He promoted a life characterized by prayer, fasting, corporate worship, and Scripture study and memorization. The same dynamics were certainly reproduced by the apostles in the life of the early church (Acts 2:42ff).

"Superficiality is the curse of our age," writes Richard Foster. "The desperate need today is not for a greater number of intelligent people, or gifted people, but for deep people."[8] An education that is Christian seeks to cultivate spiritual depth. Indeed, the program of learning that claims to be Christian is decidedly incomplete without an inner life that consciously emulates the spiritual foundation of Jesus' life and teaching.

Third, the teaching style of Jesus was characterized by *the dynamic of evangelism*. Again, we cannot hope to instruct in the fullest sense of the Christian faith without bathing our lessons in the context of outreach. In fact, evangelism has been called by many the "heartbeat of theology." Our task as teachers is to make known the Good News and to train others to do the same. Sadly, we have been rather lax in this educational task. One prominent evangelist notes that in spite of the combined efforts of all lay and professional programs in churches and parachurch agencies, it takes 1,000 Christians an average of 365 days a year to win one person to Christ. But who is to blame? Have our laity been taught how to communicate the Gospel? Have they been introduced by word and deed to the importance Scripture places on "going, preaching, and discipling?" Jesus the Teacher is intent on having us educate in such a way that the Good News does not remain unheard.

Today, more and more educational programs are beginning to concentrate on this aspect of evangelism. For instance, they have seen that the small group is the most natural and adaptable strategy for including and eventually assimilating those interested in the faith. Reproduction of evangelistic efforts, the pundits are beginning to tell us, is virtually impossible without active small clusters of believers reaching out and involving others. Small groups are both a terrific evangelistic and educational tool. Dr. Richard Myers suggests that "there is a correlation between the number of small groups and attendance in churches. The number of . . . classes determined how many persons can participate in the church school. . . . More classes, larger attendance; fewer classes, smaller attendance. As the number of classes are increased or decreased, so does the attendance increase or decrease."[9]

Consequently, George Hunter recognizes that there is a strong correlation between a church's "number of units [small groups] and its membership strength." Also, he notes that new units are generally more reproductive than old units. His observations lead him to believe that a normal church, for instance, should have:

8 groups per 100 members - to be structured for significant growth

7 groups per 100 members - to be structured for growth

6 groups per 100 members - to be structured for maintenance to slight growth

5 groups per 100 members - to be structured for maintenance or membership decline

4 or fewer groups per 100 members - to be structured for decline.[10]

A small group is usually defined in these instances as a face to face fellowship of 10-30 people who meet together at least monthly. In any case, more and more research is beginning to say much the same thing. Small groups, willing to reach out, include, and love others are one of the best evangelistic tools.

Closely related is the fourth piece of our wholistic pie. It is the issue of *social action*. In Jesus' educational comings and goings with the Twelve, few things are more evident than this aspect of His activity. His disciples were constantly with Him, aiding in His ministries of preaching, healing, and compassion. Jesus demanded, in quite vivid terms, that those associated with Him emulate these acts of kindness (see Matt. 25:31ff). It was not an option; social mercy was an essential part of the education Jesus provided His disciples. The early Church got the message. Testimony from its followers, and from those who definitely were not, attests to this. Julian the Apostate, while trying to stamp out Christianity in the Roman Empire

THE MASTER PLAN OF TEACHING

(361–363), noted with disgust that "The godless Galileans (Christians) feed not only their poor but ours also!"[11] Tertullian, writing quite a bit earlier, seemed to agree: "It is our care for the helpless, our practice of lovingkindness, that brands us in the eyes of many of our opponents."[12] The evangelism of the early Christians brought a message of good news for the whole man—body and soul. E. Stanley Jones remarked that, "Evangelism without social action is like a body without a soul. Social action without evangelism is like a soul without a body. One is a ghost and the other a corpse . . . and we don't want either one!"[13] Evangelism, Jesus style, was reaching down and lifting people up to the healing touch of our Lord wherever needed—in body or spirit.

Fifth, the instruction of the Master focused on *loving fellowship*. The disciples walked and talked together and, in the end, were told quite explicitly to love one another just as they had been loved by their teacher Jesus. It was a love

> . . . of shared meals,
> . . . of shared encouragement,
> . . . of shared challenge,
> . . . of shared finances,
> . . . of shared trials,
> . . . of shared lessons,
> . . . of shared prayers, and
> . . . of shared dreams.

In essence, they were called together in love as an educational alliance on the move for the cause of the kingdom. And the caring community which they shared proved irresistible to the men and women around them.

Jesus expected, even commanded, that His disciples reproduce their faith in others. But His was a wholistic faith, combining each of the five elements described above. I doubt that Jesus prepared a daily lesson plan to ensure the inclusion of each ingredient. Biblical truth, prayer and the formation of the inner life, evangelism, and social action, fellowship and family were so much a "package deal" that they overlapped and became one in the life and work of the Master Teacher. That is the kingdom vision for our lives as well, and the lives of those individuals in whom we invest our love, time, and energy.

One of my colleagues in ministry shared, in a seminar, the idea that all of these aspects should be a priority for small groups such as Sunday School classes. At the end of his presentation he opened up the meeting for questions and a woman in the back row of the church stood up and objected, "We don't have time!" She took everyone, including herself, by surprise, as evidenced by the moment of silence that followed. After making that admission, her eyes welled up with tears. Recovering, she confessed, "I guess what I am saying is that we don't really have time to be Christian."

Christlike education means that we take the time.

This chapter began with a Scripture passage commonly termed "the Great Commission." To be sure, Rabbi Jesus' call to "make disciples" is the greatest of all commands. But a friend once challenged, "That passage ought to be termed the 'Unfulfilled Commission.' As far as we are concerned, there is not much that is too great about it." He was acknowledging a fact that we all too often forget: The teaching style of Jesus belongs in our lives now, wherever we are. To simply label Jesus' command to evangelize "Great" is not laudatory. The words must be put into action.

Some time ago I became interested in the term "life" and looked it up in several encyclopedias and dictionaries. Most lists of the characteristics of life contain the following attributes: 1. Metabolism (assimilation and transformation of food as a usable source of energy), 2. Excretion of material no longer useful, 3. Response to external stimuli, and 4. Reproduction.

All of these would make for excellent transference to the spiritual; for example, the spiritually alive assimilate and transform the Word of God (our food) into a usable source of energy. As I scanned various reference books, however, one attribute surfaced continually—and it corresponds to the last characteristic mentioned above.

Living things *reproduce*. The consequence of not reproducing is extinction. What is true physically is overwhelmingly the case spiritually. The Great Commission is fulfilled by living persons. More to the point, the mandate of Jesus requires living teachers—those, in essence, who base their lives and ministries on the command to make disciples. The bottom-line questions are these: Are we living teachers? Are we willing to pay the price to be instruments of God to build lives of godliness in our students? Will we pattern ourselves after the Master Teacher? Will we take the time?

Remember from chapter 8 that Pygmalion's statue-bride, brought to life by the goddess Venus, ended up giving birth to her daughter Paphos. The statue, once it became a creation of life, immediately reproduced. In the same way, the disciples—having been brought to abundant life by Jesus through the power of the Holy Spirit—went to extreme lengths to reproduce themselves spiritually. Some scholars suggest that a day came when the apostles gathered in Jerusalem, keeping in mind Jesus' injunction to be witnesses to the ends of the earth (Acts 1:8), and divided up the world between them. In essence, they decided by lot where each would go. Ringing in their ears was Jesus' command to go and make disciples. They could never forget His dreams for them, that they might go throughout the world spreading this new Gospel of living.

They made disciples as Jesus had commanded them, despite the cost. Historical records and church tradition suggest that:

Matthew first taught and wrote in Judea before suffering martyrdom by being slain with a sword in the Ethiopian city of Nadabah.

John is thought to have founded the churches of Smyrna, Pergamos, Sardis, Philadelphia, Laodicea, and Thyatira. From Ephesus he was sent to Rome where he was ordered to be put into a cauldron of boiling oil. He somehow escaped death and was later banished to the Isle of Patmos, the only apostle to escape violent death.

Peter ministered in Antioch, Asia Minor, and Rome. He was

forced to watch his wife crucified and then was himself crucified, upside down (at his request) so as not to die as his Lord had died.

James, son of Zebedee is said to have brought the Good News of Christ to Spain (today he is their patron saint) and returned later to be beheaded at Jerusalem by King Herod Agrippa I.

James, son of Alphaeus was selected to oversee the churches of Jerusalem and was later beaten, stoned, and killed with a fuller's club.

Philip, great luminary of Asia, was eventually martyred there by hanging in Hierapolis.

Bartholomew carried the Gospel to several countries and propagated his translation of the Gospel of Matthew in India. He was, according to tradition, arrested, beaten with clubs, flayed alive, and then crucified.

Andrew was a Christian communicator to many lands—Cappadocia, Bithynia, Galatia, Byzantium and Scythia. In Achaia in Greece, in the town of Patras, Andrew died a martyr, scourged with a rod, fastened to a cross, and left to die.

Thomas went to the Parthians, Medes, Persians, Carmanians, Hyrcanians, Bacatrians, and Magians and eventually died (by the thrust of a spear) in India.

Thaddeus supposedly taught the Gospel in several places and was eventually crucified at Edessa in A.D. 72.

Simon (the Zealot) relayed the Christian message to Mauritania, Africa, and in England where he was crucified.

Matthias (who replaced Judas) was a teacher who for his boldness was stoned and then beheaded in Jerusalem.

While the exact locations or circumstances of the Apostles' deaths may be in dispute, the overwhelming opinion of scholars is that the reproduction of the Christ through their lives was no easy matter. They were forced to give their lives for their faith. Jesus was right. "Wisdom is vindicated by all her children" (Luke 7:35). Justification for the enormous amount of time Jesus invested in these men is found in the spread of the Gospel to "Jerusalem, and in all Judea and Samaria, and even to the remotest part of the earth" (Acts 1:8).

Beginning Steps . . .

1. *Identify two or three persons whom you might begin training to reproduce their spiritual lives.*

2. *Does your teaching style more closely reflect the sect or the ecclesia paradigm? List the strengths and weaknesses of your style as they relate to these paradigms and Jesus' style. What changes can you make for more effective teaching?*

3. *Rank the five elements of wholistic discipleship—knowledge, devotional life, evangelism, social action, and fellowship—in order of their emphasis in your teaching. Identify steps you can take to achieve a balance.*

*In this messed up world, the only children who are
going to make something of themselves are those who
come from strong parents or those who have
had a strong teacher. One or
the other. Or both.*

—Marva Collins

*All things both great and small . . .
He made and loveth all.*

—Coleridge

◗ Jesus allowed people to learn at varying
levels.

◗ We can effectively do the same, by utilizing the "funnel strategy" in our
homes, churches, and schools.

◗ We must not allow the "cult of efficiency" to deter us—there are no "instant
Christians."

CHAPTER ELEVEN

MAKING DISCIPLES AT ALL LEVELS: A STRATEGY FOR HOME, CHURCH, AND SCHOOL

The underlying genius of Jesus' teaching style and strategy was His instruction in the small group. This group consisted of the disciples with whom Jesus expended most of His time and educational energy. But such small group membership is not the only manner in which to be a disciple.

Remember that disciple means "learner." Even in Jesus' day, being a disciple didn't necessarily mean being numbered among the small band of men which surrounded Him. There were other disciples—even if not called precisely by that name—who followed and spread the news of Christ after His departure. One such group was known as the Seventy, whom Scripture says Jesus also appointed to learn and serve (Luke 10:1). The Gospels mention a number of women who followed close behind and were supporters of Christ, including Mary Magdalene, Joanna, Susanna, and many others (Luke 8:1-3). There were learners like Mark, who later penned an account of the life of Jesus. And, of course, there were those who might best be called the "crowd," the "masses," or the "multitude." Of these, Robert Coleman notes that:

He Himself continuously preached to the crowds that followed His miracle-working ministry. He taught them. He fed them when they were hungry. He healed their sick and cast out demons among them. He blessed their children. Sometimes the whole day would be spent ministering to their needs, even to the extent that He had "no leisure so much as to eat" (Mark 6:31). In every way possible Jesus manifested to the masses of humanity a genuine concern. These were the people that He came to save—He loved them, wept over them, and finally died to save them from their sin. [1]

Yet as Jesus' teaching ministry embraced the larger context of followers, it also narrowed—even within the small group. For instance, within the company of the committed twelve there appear to be three with whom Jesus had a more intimate relationship. Searching the Scriptures one sees that Peter, James, and John, seem to enjoy a unique relationship with the Master. They are with Jesus at strategic points—at the healing of Jairus' daughter, at the Mount of Transfiguration, at Gethsemane in Jesus' final hours, at other teaching moments of import. I have heard a few teachers try to carry this narrowing process one step further. They assert that perhaps John, called "the disciple whom Jesus loved" (John 13:23; 19:26; 20:2; 21:7, 20) and the one who reclined on Jesus' breast during the Last Supper, may have had a closer and more special personal relationship with Him than any of the others.

Clearly, there were varying levels and entry points for disciples in the ministry of the Master Teacher. His was a strategy that encouraged and educated disciples, however intensely they decided to be involved. The following inverted triangle (Page 207) shows what must have been a deliberate strategy on Jesus' part to reach the world with the Good News of God. [2]

The accounts of Jesus' ministry show no sign of complaint from those who were not included in the progressively narrowing levels of the triangle. I attribute this apparent harmony to three factors. First, there seems to be a greater degree of responsibility and time commitment associated with the more selective levels of the educational schema. By a natural process this eliminated many from proceeding with the deepening challenge of more intensive discipleship. Second, not everyone

Jesus' Outreach

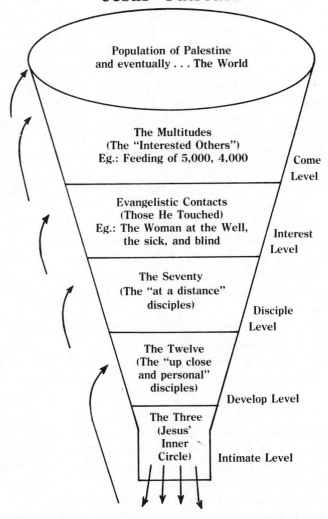

Population of Palestine
and eventually . . . The World

The Multitudes
(The "Interested Others")
Eg.: Feeding of 5,000, 4,000

Come Level

Evangelistic Contacts
(Those He Touched)
Eg.: The Woman at the Well,
the sick, and blind

Interest Level

The Seventy
(The "at a distance"
disciples)

Disciple Level

The Twelve
(The "up close
and personal"
disciples)

Develop Level

The Three
(Jesus'
Inner
Circle)

Intimate Level

▲ More intensified relationships as funnel narrows, evidenced by more time and effort spent on fewer numbers.

▲ Ultimately the funnel narrows so that the disciples will be equipped to have an effect on the other levels of influence.

207

may have developed the desire to move into closer physical proximity with the Master. Perhaps with time they felt the impetus to pursue such a relationship, but the strategy of Jesus seems to leave the open option for individuals to keep at a distance until they were prepared to seek a closer association. Finally, there was probably a lack of jealousy among those who received less preferential treatment than did the twelve and the "inner three" because, as Coleman notes, "though they did murmur about other things, [there] is proof that where preference is shown in the right spirit and for the right reason offenses need not arise."[3]

The hope of Jesus was increasing commitment and involvement on the part of His followers. He kept the challenges before them. The initial step in the path of a follower was simply to listen. To begin to follow and accept some kingdom work would be a bigger move. Being named an apostle meant taking upon oneself special privileges and responsibilities not available to everyone. Membership in the inner circle of three entailed a relationship of such intimacy and intensity that even Peter, James, and John must have felt a mixture of marvel and fear such as few have ever known.

The question that must be examined is this: Can the educational style of Jesus work in the variety of instructional situations that exist in our Christian world? Can the objectives of the Master—holy character, priestly service, and loving community—be adapted in the context where we minister? Can the principles we've spoken to in the last several chapters work for us? The resounding answer is yes. But it is a qualified yes—if by that affirmative we mean that the principles, not necessarily the exact specifics, of His style can be adapted to our respective educational responsibilities. No situation allows an absolutely precise conversion of methodology. Therefore, the adaptation from first century Palestine to modern settings will require insight, patience, and serious thought.

Lessons for the Family

"Every home a school, every parent a teacher," writes Robert Cole, editor of the *Phi Delta Kappan*. "For better or for worse children bear the indelible stamp of their upbringing long before they are mustered into schools."[4] He is right, of course, and that is why we assert that if the methodology of Jesus has applicability anywhere, it is in the family unit.

The family was from the beginning the small group par excellence for the propagation of the faith of Israel. The sixth chapter of Deuteronomy spells this out very clearly: "Hear O Israel! The Lord is our God, the Lord is one! And you shall love the Lord your God with all your heart and with all your soul and with all your might" (vv. 4-5). Those words "all your might" are a curious sort. They are translated from the Hebrew m^e 'od commonly used in the Old Testament (298 times!) as an adverb meaning "exceedingly, greatly, or very." Only twice is it used as a noun, and here is one of those places. Although somewhat awkward in English, the translation might more appropriately be rendered "Love the Lord your God with *all your exceedingly.*" Obviously, the Lord was speaking here in unique terminology, to arrest the Israelites' attention and alert them that this was a special commandment indeed. Another interesting word use in the Shema occurs in verses 6-7. "And these words, which I am commanding you today, shall be on your heart; and you shall teach them diligently to your sons." The words here—"teach them diligently"—are translated from the Hebrew *shanan* which occurs only nine times in the Old Testament and only once in the intensive stem of the verb called the Piel. That single time is here in these verses. *Shanan* is normally translated sharpen. But used in the intensive form, as it is here, *shanan* has a stronger sense. Related etymologically to the Hebrew noun for "tooth," it could here mean to "incise, or carve into." Essentially, train your children in the law of God so that their lives are permanently and irrevocably marked by its message.

It should be noted that because this usage of *shanan* is so rare, another possible meaning has been proposed. Some scholars suggest, for instance, that if you attribute the verb to another root, the idea here denoted might be "repeat." While the linguists discuss it and try to come to some kind of consensus I am willing to strike the middle ground. These verses might easily read: "Love the Lord your God . . . with all your exceedingly! And how shall you do this? Let the law of God be on your heart, and effectually carve it into the lives of your children by continually repeating it in every activity of your day" (see vv. 7-9). With such an emphasis by God on the family at this unique juncture of revelational history, the Israelites could not but know that the family was the cornerstone for the propagation of their faith in the world.

So it is with Christianity. In fact, the best possible example, outside of the Master Himself, of what a good discipleship group should be is the nuclear family based on Deuteronomy 6:4-9. Occasionally I encounter a litany of woes about the loss of real Christian influence in America. I try to follow up such an outpouring with a question. "Why do you think this has happened to our nation?" Common answers include: (1) detrimental political leaders and policies, (2) the failure of the evangelical church to remain pure, and (3) an absence of "Billy Graham type" leaders. I can affirm such undoubtedly valid viewpoints but always find myself accenting one underlying reason for the loss of spiritual integrity whether it be in the local church, a denomination, the evangelical movement, or our nation. The number one factor is the family. Lose it and you've lost the cause. Gain it for Jesus Christ and you can't lose.

The funnel diagram can be beautifully applied to the ministry of the family. (See chart on page 211.) At the most intimate level are a few people, clustered to learn and love together. But kingdom potential is not ultimately contained within that small circle. Family members relate to one another while at the same time reaching out to people at other levels—extended family and friends, the church family, the community at large, and the world. Again, as the funnel narrows, privilege and responsibility increase. And the smaller the group, the more potentially effective the instruction rendered.

The immediate family unit is an ideal disciple-making context. The goal, of course, is for instruction received there to redemptively affect its members' conduct and outreach in ever-widening spheres of influence. Though the making of a

Family Outreach

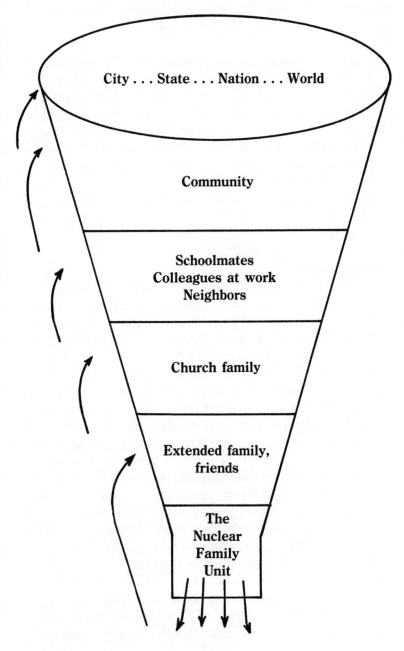

City . . . State . . . Nation . . . World

Community

Schoolmates
Colleagues at work
Neighbors

Church family

Extended family,
friends

The
Nuclear
Family
Unit

Christian family is a much more complex task than can be discussed in this brief chapter, the following guidelines should be considered by Christian couples and parents.

(1) *Make the family discipleship group your number one priority.*
In the scheduling of our time—It has been said that good parenting is spelled T-I-M-E. Current statistics note that an average father spends less than ten minutes per week in face-to-face, quality conversation with his children. (Some statistics have it below five minutes.) The fact is, families need to spend more time (quantity) and better time (quality) together. We must not excuse ourselves from spending healthy portions of time because we emphasize "quality time" with our families. If we rely merely on quality, it is a good bet that we are not spending nearly enough time.

(2) *Make proximity and presence a priority.*
Who is raising your children? Optimizing the teaching of your family requires that the parents spend large portions of time with the children. More and more, that time is being diminished as both parents, for instance, deliver their offspring to day care and march off to their respective jobs. This, in some circumstances, may need to be a consideration for certain families. But many of us need to make financial sacrifices in order to stay at home with the children. We certainly can't teach after the example of Deuteronomy 6, in all the activities of life, if we aren't there to share those experiences with our children and to take advantage of the teachable moments which arise. Even in Jesus' day the call to teach was a call to poverty.

It is high time such a position be given the esteem which it deserves. While a call to teach in Palestine was a call to poverty, it was also a position of honor. Anthony Campolo has a wonderful story about parenthood:

In reality, such roles can be noble callings. When I was on the faculty of the University of Pennsylvania, there were gatherings from time to time to which faculty members

212

brought their spouses. Inevitably, some woman lawyer or sociologist would confront my wife with the question, "And what is it that you do, my dear?" My wife, who is one of the most brilliantly articulate individuals I know, had a great response: "I am socializing two homo sapiens into the dominant values of the Judeo-Christian tradition in order that they might be instruments for the transformation of the social order into the telelogically prescribed utopia inherent in the eschaton."

When she followed that with,"And what is it that you do?" the other person's "A lawyer" answer just wasn't that overpowering.[5]

Children need incarnate parents committed to living faith full-time before their children, in the power of the Holy Spirit. It is an honor to teach as Jesus taught, but there is a price to be paid, in presence and proximity.

(3) *Strengthen the inner life and fortitude of the child.*
   Merton and Irene Strommen suggest this is done by implementing these four emphases:
   a. A close but open family life is possible when parents
      ▲ demonstrate affection in their relationship with each other,
      ▲ communicate effectively with their children and each other,
      ▲ teach responsible lifestyles through consistent, firm democratic control,
      ▲ show affection, respect, and trust in their child.

   b. Moral beliefs and purpose are encouraged by parents who
      ▲ seek to live within the universe of traditional moral beliefs,
      ▲ have a life orientation that is not overly restrictive or self-centered,
      ▲ model a life that carries responsibility for others' needs,
      ▲ help children internalize beliefs by using rational expla-

nations of right and wrong.

c. A personal, liberating faith is encouraged by parents who themselves
    ▲ have a faith that is liberating rather than restrictive,
    ▲ share experiences of faith with members of the family,
    ▲ discuss Scriptures and pray together with their family,
    ▲ model "doing the truth" by aiding those in need.

d. The support of caring people is made possible when parents
    ▲ accept the help of others,
    ▲ become part of a network of caring adults,
    ▲ seek help when their child is in trouble,
    ▲ learn methods of discipline that are consistent, firm, and fair.[6]

(4) *Read through the major principles of this book and remember that they are more readily applied within the context of the family than anywhere else.* For instance, nowhere will the power of day-to-day conversation affect the child more than in the home. A consistent, everyday example of servanthood will rub off too. Self-esteem, for the most part, is learned in the home. The words and actions of parents and guardians have dramatic impact. An incarnate—Spirit-endued, in the flesh, and full-time—parent can lay the foundation for future disciples to impact their world for Christ. Christlike education belongs in the home, if it belongs anywhere at all.

These considerations, and others which you might prayerfully add, should serve as a barometer of how the family rates as your top educational priority. Responsibly ask the following questions: What adjustments would Jesus have me make to effectively teach this small group with which He has honored me? What does His style have to say to me?

The intimacy of learning within the acceptance and security of the home is designed to make disciples who will affect the whole of society and reproduce other godly families. A frequently cited study of the descendents of Jonathan Edwards and Max Jukes illustrates this reproduction in action. Contemporaries, these men nonetheless differed in their religious beliefs and practice. Jonathan Edwards, known as a religious and moral man had, at the time of this study, 1,394 descendents from his union with a Christian wife, Sarah. Of these, there were 100 preachers and missionaries, 100 lawyers, 80 public officials, 75 army and navy officers, 65 college professors, 60 authors of prominence, 60 physicians, 30 judges, 13 college presidents, 3 United States senators, 1 vice-president of the United States, and 295 college graduates, among whom were governors of states and ministers to foreign countries.

But the power of the nuclear family works both ways. Jukes evidently was an atheist and an example of ungodly living. From his union sprang 540 known descendents whose record is less impressive. 310 died as paupers. 150 were criminals; 100, drunkards; 7, murderers; and more than half of the women were prostitutes.[7] The offspring of Jukes and his wife are a vivid reminder that what can work for good can also produce evil.

The teaching style of Jesus belongs first and foremost in the family. If it is true that the church has lost its capacity to think and act Christianly, then it is by Jesus' educational methodology actively practiced in the family that she can reclaim her vision.

Lessons for the Church

Jesus' "funnel strategy" works in and for the church. But today it is often neglected, to Christendom's loss. Thankfully, there are pockets of faithful individuals who have seen the efficacy of His approach and small movements of renewal are taking place. But too few congregations are implementing Jesus' methodology. Perhaps G.K. Chesterton was right: "The Christian ideal, it is said, has not been tried and found wanting; it has been found difficult and left untried."[8] Difficult or not, the strategy of Jesus is crucial if the church is to function as designed. His strategy provides the remedy to the unchanged lives, inactive membership, and purposelessness which plague the modern church.

Youth Group Outreach

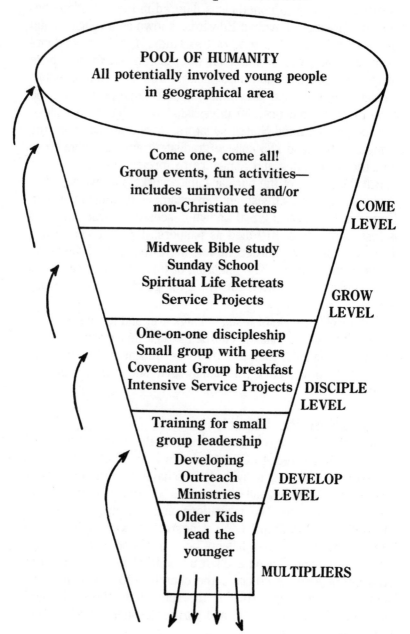

POOL OF HUMANITY
All potentially involved young people
in geographical area

Come one, come all!
Group events, fun activities—
includes uninvolved and/or
non-Christian teens

COME LEVEL

Midweek Bible study
Sunday School
Spiritual Life Retreats
Service Projects

GROW LEVEL

One-on-one discipleship
Small group with peers
Covenant Group breakfast
Intensive Service Projects

DISCIPLE LEVEL

Training for small
group leadership
Developing
Outreach
Ministries

DEVELOP LEVEL

Older Kids
lead the
younger

MULTIPLIERS

Let's take a look to see how it might work at the level of the local church. My wife was actively involved in a youth ministry which employed the funnel approach. The whole purpose of this model is to involve as many people as possible at the deepest commitment levels.

1. *The Pool of Humanity*—For Jesus, this category comprised the population of Palestine—the group of people to whom He had access; in the case of the particular youth ministry in question, all potentially involved youth in the geographical area. This classification can be particularized to your own setting: In the broadest sense, who are the people whom you are attempting to reach?

2. *Come Level* is the level of first, and broadest, outreach, requiring the lowest degree of participation. Jesus' ministry exhibited this kind of outreach to the masses, the large groups who seemed to gather wherever He appeared. The feeding of the 5,000 is a perfect example of a "Come Level" activity—the people came, heard Jesus' message, and were provided a meal.

For the youth group context, this category comprised non-threatening group events in which everyone was invited to participate, with little required besides attendance. Typical fare included lock-ins, youth group parties, group skating, and bowling—things that allowed youth group members to invite non-Christian friends along to find out that Christians can have fun. The particular ministry in which Mary was involved counted the Sunday night youth meeting, interestingly enough, at the "Come Level." Figuring the kids had enough "heavy duty" Bible teaching that day with Sunday School and two church services, the evening fellowship took a lighter approach. All grades, 7-12, met together. There was a lesson—often presented with humor—but also, games, activities, and always, refreshments.

3. *Grow Level*—Often as not, some people who enter at the "Come Level" decide to investigate further, a step which entails a measure of initiative and thus the first degree of commitment. We can see this aspect in Jesus' ministry, with both groups and individuals. Nicodemus, for instance, sought Jesus

out to get a second look. Others, in response to His proclamation and teaching, approached Jesus to ask for help and healing. The group of women who followed and ministered to Jesus must have come in through this door—hearing His message, then returning again and again until they became a part of His entourage.

In youth ministry, the fun activities mentioned above served as a draw to attract students. Many saw something they liked and were willing to become more involved, so they moved on to the "Grow Level"—attending the age-graded, Wednesday evening Bible study, which was more substantial in terms of content than the Sunday night meeting. Other typical "Grow Level" activities included Sunday School and certain special events, like retreats, which included along with the fun some Bible study and growth opportunities.

4. *Disciple Level*—As the funnel narrows, the degree of involvement increases. At the "Disciple Level," people begin to actively participate in the faith process. In Jesus' ministry we see not only the Twelve, but also the seventy who are committed to a closer relationship of obedience to Him. They follow Jesus, absorb His teaching, and are commissioned to action.

As kids in the youth group felt the need and desire to get more intentional in their relationship with Christ, "Disciple level" opportunities were open to them. They could sign up for one-on-one discipleship with a member of the youth ministry team to work on specific areas of their Christian life—Bible study, relationship with parents/siblings, prayer, witnessing—pinpointed by them in consultation with the youth minister. Youth in grades nine and above might join the Covenant Group, a Tuesday morning before-school breakfast meeting in which both adult leaders and youth shared their spiritual progress and problems. Joining this group meant a one semester, renewable commitment to come no matter what. And those who persevered to the end got to go on a special retreat at the end of the semester. Another option was to be involved in a small group of three or four people. The groups for older teens were led by youth ministry team members, while the junior highers looked to 11th and 12th graders for leadership of their groups.

5. *Develop Level*—This leads us to the "Develop Level," comprised of people who have made the commitment to be faithful followers and are being eased into roles of leadership. Jesus began this transition with the Twelve while He was still with them, giving them tasks and honing their skills so that they would be able to fulfill His later commission to make disciples.

The senior high small group leaders mentioned above, who were chosen and trained by the youth minister, are an example of the "Disciple Level" in action. They had made progressive commitments which brought them from the "Come Level" through the other stages. Now they were not only involved in the Wednesday Bible study, the Covenant Group and one-on-one discipleship with youth leaders to build their own faith and walk; they had also become Multipliers, practicing hands-on the skills they had been taught. They were learning to relate to others, to share their faith, and to prepare and lead Bible studies. And from there could be launched a whole new generation of Multipliers, people who become effective reproducers in their own Spirit-led ministries.

I have seen the above pattern work in a number of youth groups to great effect. It can work in the church at large with adaptations. Let's take a look at how. (See chart on page 221.)

First of all, a broad range of "Come Level" opportunities should be provided to welcome non-Christians or nominal participators into active fellowship in our churches. If we make the mouth of the funnel too narrow, we defeat its purpose of filtering people into the deeper life of faith. Adults might not indulge in as many "fun" activities as the youth seem to. But church sports teams (basketball, softball), potluck suppers, and other non-threatening events serve as easy entry points for the uninitiated but interested. The Sunday morning service already functions at this level in many churches. Of all the weekly services, non-believers or nominal Christians are most likely to attend this one. They come with their friends, or out of habit, or guilt, or interest in someone else who attends there. The motivations are legion. The range of attention spans present in the average morning service is just as varied. That's not to say we should just offer spiritual pablum here. Still, let's make sure people feel warmly welcomed.

They may even decide they'd like to learn more. "Grow Level" activities are already in place in most churches. Sunday School classes, Wednesday night prayer meetings, monthly men's breakfasts, and women's circles all provide opportunities to become more consistently involved, to learn, and to build relationships—all key features of the educational process.

Those who really want to go deeper and move on to the "Disciple Level" may feel thwarted in some congregations. This is where many churches cease to offer the kind of opportunities for increased commitment, learning, and growth. We often don't have programs in place that can be adapted to meet the "Disciple Level" need. Organizing small group home Bible studies and pairing interested disciples one-on-one with more mature Christians are two solutions. The pastor may find the elders, deacons, cabinet, or other leadership team to be a natural small group for this more intensified relationship. Keep your eyes open, too, because this is the place where you will find and form future Multipliers—people whom you can guide through the "Develop Level," gradually giving them leadership responsibilities for the spiritual oversight of others. And as the Multipliers increase, there will be more people to step in and meet the need of those in the Disciple (and other) levels.

In his poem *Lycidas* John Milton penned these mournful words: "The hungry sheep look up and are not fed."[9] No sadder indictment could be made upon a church or family than that. A program like that described above can be adapted to ensure that sheep in search of spiritual food will close their mouths on something that satisfies.

The major lessons are these:

(1) Disciples are made—at some extent—at each level of the funnel.

(2) The church should provide varying levels of growth.

(3) Leadership should be produced that can impact levels of less intensity.

Church Outreach

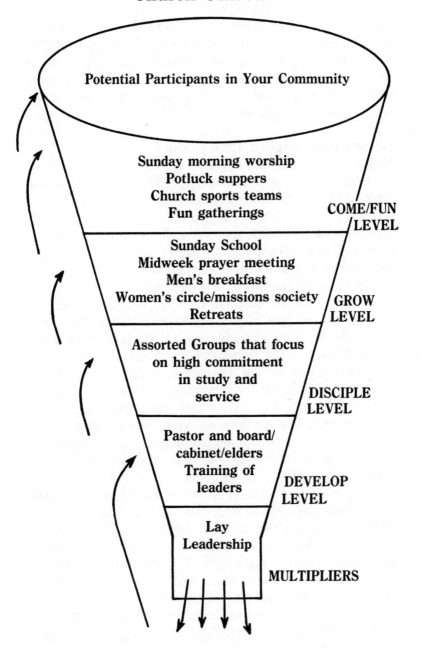

Potential Participants in Your Community

Sunday morning worship
Potluck suppers
Church sports teams
Fun gatherings

COME/FUN LEVEL

Sunday School
Midweek prayer meeting
Men's breakfast
Women's circle/missions society
Retreats

GROW LEVEL

Assorted Groups that focus
on high commitment
in study and
service

DISCIPLE LEVEL

Pastor and board/
cabinet/elders
Training of
leaders

DEVELOP LEVEL

Lay
Leadership

MULTIPLIERS

(4) *Intentional* effort must be made to *optimize* each level for God's kingdom.

The last point is critical. Many churches use the funnel strategy. But too often it is not an *intentional* emulation of "the master plan," or an effort to maximize each level to "make disciples." We must be sure to reflect His model and work to impact our communities with dramatic effect as we employ Jesus' example of education.

Lessons for Higher Education

Eighteen years after the Pilgrims set foot on Plymouth Rock, the Puritans founded the famous and oldest Ivy League school, Harvard University. Records of that institution's inception are telling: "Let every student be plainly instructed and earnestly pressed to consider well, the main end of his life and studies is to know God and Jesus Christ which is eternal life, John 17:3, and therefore to lay Christ in the bottom, as the only foundation of all sound knowledge and learning."[10]

Similarly, Yale was begun in 1701 by Christians in the Connecticut region. The impact of the First Great Awakening caused the establishment of evangelical Princeton in New Jersey in 1746. In 1754 Dartmouth launched out with a strong missionary thrust in New Hampshire. Under a royal charter from King George III, the school's specified objective was to reach the Indian tribes and educate and Christianize English youth as well. The list goes on. With the exception of one, every collegiate institution founded in the New World colonies prior to the Revolutionary War was established by and for some branch of the Christian Church.[11]

Such are the beginnings of American higher education. Obviously, much has changed since then, perhaps these particular institutions being cases in point. But even with present-day evangelical colleges and seminaries, I wonder if we haven't ventured far from a "Jesus style of learning." If our Christian institutions today aim to adopt objectives like those of the primitive Harvard, then we must not only accept the end but the means. To approach the main end of knowing "God and Jesus Christ which is eternal life" and laying "Christ in the bottom, as the only foundation of all sound knowledge and learning"—we had better accept His mode of education.

Elton Trueblood, in his book *The Idea of a College*, described one strand of the higher educational scene as he perceived it in 1959:

> *It is still standard experience for the professor and his students to be genuine friends, not ashamed to be seen together, for most teaching is such that there is a truly personal relationship between teacher and taught. . . . Membership in a college involves far more than attendance at classes, and this is as it should be.*
>
> *Ideally, the members of a college, both teachers and taught, work together, think together, play together, and pray together.*[12]

I fear that this "idea of a college" is becoming as dated as Trueblood's decades-old words. To teach and learn by working, thinking, playing, and praying together is education in the tradition of Jesus. Sadly, for the most part, we have abandoned this ideal. Too often we live in an impersonal world where teachers and students drive to campus, spend a few hours, and quickly depart for jobs and families. When a teacher sees an opportunity to initiate significant one-on-one interaction with a student, the temptation is often great—in the face of committee meetings, pressure to publish, and the never-ending pursuit of lecture material—to dismiss the thought. Our education becomes one of much information and precious little formation.

But if most institutions have lost that intimate touch, we must remind ourselves that the loss has not been total. There are always bright spots on the dim horizon. I attended a seminary where all the pressures of a prestigious evangelical graduate school were alive and well. Professors were expected to shoulder a substantial course load, publish, advise, attend committee meetings, and be prepared to evaluate their respective departments for the accreditation association. The instructors found themselves as busy as you could expect professionals in any vocation to be. Not surprisingly, many of the professors felt caught in a time bind and had difficulty finding hours enough to invest in a few students as Jesus might have done.

I remember three notable exceptions. Each of these professors somehow made the time to be with students on a weekly, covenant basis in their offices and homes, at lunch, and in the field of ministry. One was a theology professor with a penchant for strict spiritual disciplines and accountability. Another was into human development and Christian education. Yet another concentrated on New Testament exegesis and social justice. Each had his own field, personality, and agenda. Once students had been on campus awhile and discovered that these professors were available for extra-curricular interaction and informal small group relationships, the three teachers were inundated with requests to be involved.

The price was monumental in terms of time and effort. One couldn't help but notice that these professors were constantly with students—loving, discussing, arguing, laughing, and eating. Such involvement means less time for yourself and your other duties. There is less solitude and thus fewer opportunities for individual pursuits. But if you could see these professors in action you would know that they are bent on impacting students' lives intellectually, emotionally, spiritually, and developmentally. The normal classroom/advisor role expected of all professors was not enough for these men. They wanted more than that and sacrificed more for that. And they got results. As I look at graduates from that seminary across the United States and even the world, I find that the majority of the most active and fruitful have been profoundly influenced by one of these men. As students gathered with these teachers in offices, lunchrooms, ministry, and homes, their lives were qualitatively changed. These professors have found that a "Jesus style" methodology works. But professors and teachers who employ these tactics soon find that they are a rare commodity.

Several years ago the *Christian Science Monitor* ran a feature on Larry Axel, a professor of religion and philosophy at

Relationships in Higher Education

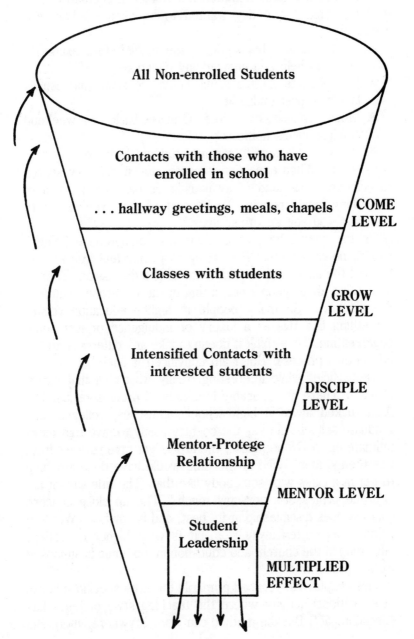

All Non-enrolled Students

Contacts with those who have
enrolled in school

... hallway greetings, meals, chapels

COME
LEVEL

Classes with students

GROW
LEVEL

Intensified Contacts with
interested students

DISCIPLE
LEVEL

Mentor-Protege
Relationship

MENTOR LEVEL

Student
Leadership

MULTIPLIED
EFFECT

Purdue University. It was an invigorating piece on education and caught my attention immediately. Axel, it seemed to me, modeled what I one day wanted to be as a teacher. For instance:

▲ He telephones his students the night before exams to offer his help and answer any questions.
▲ He conducts classes in his home, sessions that usually last well past midnight.
▲ Most summers, he invites graduates back for a weekend seminar in his home.
▲ He writes letters to former students every day.

Says Axel: "When education is successful, it probably serves to achieve some kind of awakening or blossoming forth of something inside people. To be part of that, you've got to integrate yourself into their lives."

On the course he teaches from his home (one evening a week), he comments: "It's set up so people feel free to stay beyond the allotted time and continue the discussion. There's something about people not sitting in the classroom watching the clock. . . . So many people in higher education regard something like this as a luxury or indulgence or just some sugarcoating. They think it doesn't make any difference to the educational process. But I am convinced it does."[13]

The article, while interesting, really wasn't all that earth-shaking. There are probably hundreds of professors just like Axel tucked away in high schools, churches, colleges, and graduate schools all over the country ready to give that extra intimate effort. Nonetheless, the article got rave reviews from this then-student, who at the time would have done anything to get in a class with somebody like that. The title says it all: "Purdue professor's personal touch." The up close concern characterizes discipleship at its best, and is what our Western culture has gotten away from. It is what higher education, education in the church, and education in the home is supposed to be all about.

This chapter has focused primarily on three specific spheres of educational activity where the teaching style of Jesus has special impact. But the method can work anywhere where His disciples decide to apply it with the aid of the Holy Spirit. I have seen the model in place in public schools through such programs as the Fellowship of Christian Athletes. I have heard of businesses where a core group of employees is trying to redemptively affect their workplace for the kingdom. There are a number of examples of local, state, and national governments meeting together for learning and encouragement. The point is this: We must find out where the Lord would have us engaged on a day-to-day basis and then ask for divine guidance as to how such a methodology can work right in our own backyards.

The Cult of Efficiency

The teaching style of Jesus needs to be applied at every point where Christian discipleship is an issue and where real education is the goal. If we truly desire to produce earnest workers for a worldwide movement of redemptive change, then we need to take seriously not only the fundamental message of the Master, but also His fundamental method.

To do so entails acknowledging the culture in which we live and work and understanding the possible battles ahead in implementing this particular educational strategy. One of the primary pitfalls that puts this methodology at risk is outlined in a book by Raymond Callahan entitled *Education and the Cult of Efficiency*. In it he describes what he considers the downfall of American education in the twentieth century.

Early in this century educators were attacked by critics who, like their counterparts in business and industry, asked the question, "How can we get the best product for the lowest cost, and *fast?*" Frederick Taylor, the guru of scientific management, noted that his principles should be "applied with equal force to all social activities: to the management of our homes ... to our universities ..."[14] Indeed, says Callahan, Taylor's wish came true. Efficiency experts began to apply principles of scientific management to the home, family, church, and education. Their efforts took on ridiculous dimensions when, for instance, the experts addressed the efficiency of the average household.

> *. . . the editors of the* Outlook *began a series of articles on "Home Efficiency." In announcing the series the problem was introduced with some pertinent questions such as: "Does your home pay? Does it make a fair return on the investment of time and strength and money that is put into it? As a factory for the production of citizenship is it a success?" . . . "Cannot the management of the average household be conducted as a business proposition?" . . . [One of the writers] suggested that the "management" work out ten or twelve standardized meals each with a standard content, a standard procedure, and a standard time. On the question of time studies he demonstrated how they could be used in the making of biscuits, which process he broke down into eighteen operations with the time allotment (in seconds) provided for each step. For those servants who developed into efficient first-class workers, and who, for example, did not waste seconds gazing out of the window while putting the biscuits into the oven, he suggested an appropriate reward.* [15]

Extensive and silly applications of the radical efficiency model were made to the church and schools. Callahan writes that it was not that some of the ideas from the business world might not have been used to advantage in the sphere of education, but that the wholesale adoption of the basic values was a serious mistake where the primary purpose was education. President Richard Lyman of Stanford University probably says it best: "It won't do us much good to have the whole system beautifully organized and transformed into a cost account's paradise, if the heart and soul have been squeezed out of it." [16]

While we may have rebounded somewhat from the overzealous and inappropriate attempts at efficiency of the early part of the century, I do not think that we have escaped the problem entirely. Laments A. W. Tozer in his article on "The Inadequacy on 'Instant Christianity' ":

> *Instant Christianity came in with the machine age. Men invented machines for two purposes. They wanted to get*

important work done more quickly and easily than they could do it by hand, and they wanted to get the work over with so they could give their time to pursuits more to their liking, such as loafing or enjoying the pleasures of the world. Instant Christianity now serves the same purposes in religion. . . . It fails to understand the true nature of the Christian life, which is not static but dynamic and expanding. It overlooks the fact that a new Christian is a living organism as certainly as a new baby is, and must have nourishment and exercise to assure normal growth. . . . Instant Christianity is twentieth century orthodoxy. I wonder whether the man who wrote Philippians 3:7-16 would recognize it as the faith for which he finally died. I am afraid he would not. [17]

Re-read the above passage, mentally substituting "Christian education" for the word "Christianity," and you'll get the point as it relates specifically to our struggles toward Christlike teaching today. Suffice it to say, there is no instant Christlikeness, and a program bent on meeting the objectives of His kingdom must be willing to take the time.

As products of Western culture, we harbor within a deepset urge to do things well, and quickly. But education with the goals of holy character, priestly service, and caring community cannot be produced on demand, with strictly regimented procedures and in short periods of time. We must look to the Master, not the efficiency experts, for our methods. And His method requires time, effort, patience, intense relationships, and all of our energy. It requires, as Tozer reminds us, "nourishment and exercise." There is a price for God to mold lives through our teaching.

Beginning Steps. . . .

1. List your priorities for family, church, and/or school — those places where you have educational responsibilities. With a pocket calendar, schedule specific weekly time commitments for these activities. Once the schedule is designed and is properly balanced with kingdom priorities, seek some accountability in order to stick to it.

2. *Make a copy of the funnel diagram (or use one of those in the book). To the left of each level list individuals and/or existing groups in your educational situation which fit in that category.*

3. *On the right column of the paper, write an objective beside each level. Brainstorm ideas and activities which would facilitate the accomplishment of that objective and list them.*

*Thomas More: Be a teacher. You'd be a fine teacher, perhaps
even a great one.*
Richard Rich: And if I were, who would know it?
More: You, your friends, your pupils, God. Not a bad company.

—Robert Bolt, *A Man For All Seasons*

*Whoever keeps and teaches them [the commandments] he
shall be called great in the kingdom of heaven.*

—Jesus

The Master Plan of Teaching . . .

♦ Takes plenty of patient work,
♦ Requires the help and guidance of the
Educating Spirit, and
♦ is needed this hour.

CHAPTER TWELVE

FINALE

There Barbara Walters stood, in front of the huge American flag staring prophetically into the television camera and hence into the homes of millions. Her tone was foreboding.

"The alarm has sounded," she began. "The clock is ticking. But most of us are still asleep."

"What clock?" the viewing audience asked. The masses leaned forward to find out what in the world was so wrong. An epidemic of an unknown disease? Rampant lawlessness? Bombs in our backyard?

Not exactly. Walters was doing a program on American education, or lack of education, as the case may be. American youth are unbelievably ignorant, it is suggested, on a variety of fronts—math, geography, reading, and writing skills. And it doesn't stop there. Values have plummeted. Our youngsters have few goals, a lack of discipline, and inevitably, no future for an increasing number of those with diplomas. We are becoming, Walters predicts, "a generation of undisciplined cultural barbarians."[1]

What Walters has suggested for American public education, some are predicting for Christian education in the church, home, and school. Educational pundits, within the church, have suggested that we are slowly becoming more ignorant of basic biblical facts, less likely to act on the facts we do know, and concerned only with our own small worlds. We have developed, in essence, a character-less, service-less, community-less faith.

We need courageous educators who will stand up and begin the task of looking in Scripture and finding out how He would have us educate. Implementation will take not only courage, but hard work as well. To remind ourselves of that, perhaps is tantamount to sizing up Jesus' challenge to His disciples to "deny yourself, take up your cross, and follow." Let there be no illusions, the chore of education Jesus-style is not easy. But as with most things of excellence, it is worth the effort.

A Teaching Style That Takes Work

E. Stanley Jones was delivering a series of lectures at St. Stephen's College, Delhi, when someone approached him and asked if he would like to meet "Mr. Gandhi." It was to be the first of his many contacts with Gandhi and the one which he says "brought me the most unalloyed joy of all the contacts through the years." Jones walked into a room where Gandhi was seated on his bed, surrounded by papers. He rose and greeted the missionary with his contagious smile. But Jones wasted no time in getting to his agenda. Moments like these were too precious to waste on pleasantries. He went right to the issue for which he wanted an answer. "How can we make Christianity naturalized in India . . . What would you, as one of the Hindu leaders of India, tell me, a Christian, to do in order to make this possible?" Gandhi responded with directness. "First, I would suggest that all of you Christians, missionaries and all, must begin to live more like Jesus Christ."[2]

Even from a Hindu that is profound Christian advice. I wonder if we in educational circles shouldn't respond in much the same manner. How can we change our church, our nation, our world? How can we educate people for kingdom values and redemptive directions? The answer resounds throughout the centuries since Jesus the Teacher walked the dusty roads of Palestine. The command from Scripture is that we must begin to teach more like Jesus Christ.

That will take change, and most change is excruciatingly
hard. In February of 1985, the United News of India reported
the death of a young boy who had been raised by wolves. The
boy had evidently been discovered in 1976 in the company of
three wolf cubs. UNI reported that when found "Ramu," as he
came to be known, was walking on all fours, had matted hair,
had grown long nails, and his palms, elbows, and knees were
calloused, like the pads of a wolf's paws. He was accustomed
to eating raw meat like his wolf companions and after his
capture, still attracted by it, Ramu would frequently sneak out
to attack chickens in the neighborhood.

After being captured he was handed over to Mother Teresa's Missionaries of Charity who taught him how to bathe and
wear clothes. Despite their efforts, however, the sisters never succeeded in teaching him to speak. In his twenties, Ramu
developed cramps, failed to respond to medical treatment, and
died. Here was a boy—created a human being—who had fallen
among wolves and become so naturalized into a wolf mindset,
diet, and values that he found it difficult to revert to a human
perspective, which seemed unusually foreign to him.[3]

In a sense, every Christian conversion repeats that story.
We were created by and for God—to be in fellowship with
Him—but have so accommodated ourselves to a sin nature and
environment that we find conversion to our intended holy and
Christian state to be difficult. Could the same be said for the
Christian educator? Have we, for so long, developed and practiced methodologies that are derived from other sources so
that a Christological model appears foreign to us? If so, it is
time to change, however difficult. It is time to become the
teachers we were initially meant to be.

I have a series of teaching sets which work off the old
Rolaids commercial. If you remember, the ad asks, "How do
you spell relief?" The answer: R-O-L-A-I-D-S! My lessons
pose the question, "How do you spell Christianity?" I use
several spellings, but the first is simply C-H-A-N-G-E! In
order to be in God's will we must change. That is why Jesus
comes proclaiming "Repent!" The word literally means
change, and the message is that if we are ever going to be

who we were meant to be, it will take a change.

So it is with teaching. To achieve the ultimate impact with our lives, we need to change and conform to Jesus' example. We must begin aligning our approach to education with His teaching model and recognize that for many of us, at least initially, this will require arduous effort. It is not something that comes as naturally as we would wish. Worse, the tendency of sinful people is to forego the change and work necessary to be realigned with the Master. Nonetheless, such labor is imperative if we are to be the best we can be. The words of Jesus are inescapable: "If anyone wishes to come after Me, let him deny himself, and take up his cross, and follow Me" (Matt. 16:24).

Other educators have expressed similar insights. Aristotle, for instance, was on target when he said that "the heights of great men were not attained by sudden flight."[4] In *Theogony* (ca. 700 B.C.), Hesiod made the following statement that speaks to the difficulty of attaining excellence in any field: "Badness comes easily, in quantity. The road is smooth and it lies close by. But in front of excellence the immortal gods have put sweat, and rough and steep is the way to it, and rough at first. But when you get to the top it is easy, even though it is hard."[5] A quotation from Tibetan Buddhist literature proclaims that, "If you desire ease, forsake learning. If you desire learning, forsake ease. How can the man at his ease acquire knowledge, and how can the earnest student enjoy ease?"

Excellence in teaching, as in any endeavor, takes work, vision, time, and patience. Nevertheless, the hope of this book is the same at the end as it was in the beginning—that with our lives and methodologies we will "fix our eyes upon Jesus, the author and perfecter of our faith" (Heb. 12:2, NIV). In His teaching example we find all that we were meant to do and be as educators. He is the only way to our objectives. The "master plan of teaching" is the only way to communicate the holy and happy lives He intends for us.

Dr. Benjamin Bloom has suggested in a recent study that of the exceptional young talents that his research team encountered, educators were paramount: "No one reached the limits of learning in a talent field on his or her own. Families and teachers were crucial at every point along the way to excellence. . . . What the families and teachers do at different times and how they do it clearly sets the stage for exceptional learning . . . "⁶

Christianity, if understood aright, is an "exceptional" calling. But living the level of life that Christ desires for us requires good teaching and good teachers. Without that, there is no exceptional Christian living. That is why we are called to take the task of learning from Jesus seriously. The Master Educator has much to share with us. His way is the best, regardless how much effort it may take.

The Role of the Educating Spirit

It would be a grave error to close this volume without mentioning the role of the Holy Spirit. Even those disciples who had enjoyed the physical proximity of Jesus were expected to receive and learn from the Helper, the Holy Spirit. Jesus said, "These things I have spoken to you, while abiding with you. But the Helper, the Holy Spirit, whom the Father will send in My name, He will teach you all things, and bring to your remembrance all that I said to you" (John 14:25-26). Combine the teaching presence of the Spirit with the ongoing intercession of both the Spirit (Rom. 8:27) and the Son (Heb. 7:25), and you have a combination of content, methodology, and spiritual undergirding that, joined with a willing and teachable educator, has explosive potential.

Some people are confused about emulating Jesus as teacher, for He was God; we are merely the people created in His image. Jesus was 100 percent God, 100 percent human; but we are mere mortals. How do we fit into the scheme of educating like Him?

I have always thought of it like this: What Jesus filled up in both His divinity and humanity is today met in the combination of the divine (the Holy Spirit who teaches and guides) and the human (our role, to be Christlike examples).

The potential of the contemporary teaching style represented in the following diagram is enviable. If utilized after the

THE MASTER PLAN OF TEACHING

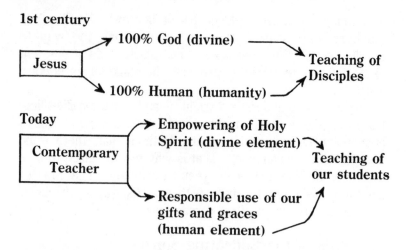

example of Jesus, one can expect from this pattern more than just good Sunday School classes and effective schools. A few teachers, bent on wholeheartedly employing His method, will start a revolution. This powerful movement will be one of love, service, and action—recalling a similar revolution recorded in the Book of Acts. We are called to be teachers like Jesus. We will be held accountable for our faithfulness to that task.

Plutarch, who lived and wrote during the early years of the infant church (46–120), wrote in his *Moralia* concerning "The Education of Children": "Now to put into effect all the suggestions which I have given is the province of prayer, perhaps, or exhortation. And even to follow zealously the majority of them demands good fortune and much careful attention, but to accomplish this lies within the capability of man."[7]

A good education—following the teaching style of Jesus—is indeed within the capabilities of man. It takes prayer, exhortation, zeal, and careful attention. But God will grant us all that we need if we eagerly and truly desire to "make disciples of all the nations" as He demonstrated and commanded. One of my favorite portions of Scripture is directly after the ascension of Christ when two men in white clothing appear beside the apostles as they gaze heavenward. The men in white had a great line: "Men of Galilee, why do you stand looking into the sky?"

(Acts 1:11) It was no time to stand and watch the clouds. It was time to prepare for the coming of the Spirit and to win a world for the message of Jesus.

Making their way to the Upper Room, the disciples devoted themselves to prayer as their Master had so frequently done and enjoyed the fellowship of other believers. When the day of Pentecost came the Spirit filled them, and from that moment they were never the same. Their immediate actions in the second chapter of Acts are telling.

▲ They communicated in language that all could understand (quite a goal for educators!).
▲ They boldly proclaimed the Word of God.
▲ The newly founded church's fellowship, breaking of bread, corporate prayer, and teaching took on a new power.
▲ There was a feeling of awe in the air.
▲ Wonders and signs were taking place.
▲ Personal belongings were shared in order to meet the needs of the whole body.
▲ Corporate worship took on new meaning, and houses were filled with people eager to know more about this Jesus.
▲ They praised God, found favor with all people, and daily increased in number.

This was Christian education at its best!

That is what we can expect to happen when people experience the teaching style of Jesus, the infilling of the Holy Spirit, and the ongoing prayers of the Godhead. We can expect normal Christian living, the kind found in the first chapters of Acts. Accommodating ourselves to anything less is subnormal.

In *Family Portrait* (Act III) Leban asks Mary of Nazareth, "Has anyone ever tried it—to live the way He taught?" Mary replies, "I don't think so." And Leban responds, "Might be interesting to see what would happen if they did."[8] The question might be asked today, "Does anybody ever teach the way He taught?" It would be interesting, indeed, to see what would happen if we did! The task is not too daunting. We can, if we will!

Finis

Writer Philip Yancey tells about the time he visited a personal counselor on a blustery Chicago day. Hearing that the pastor had participated in the liberation of the Dachau concentration camp, Yancey decided to reverse roles with the man and ask the questions. The pastor, for the next 20 minutes or so, reluctantly recounted the sights, the sounds, and even the horrifying smells that greeted his rescue unit as they walked through the gates of Dachau. His account described stacks of neatly laid bodies in boxcars piled up like firewood. The primary job of the pastor that day was to pick up each body and carry it to a designated area. The pastor recalls:

> *I couldn't believe it the first time we came across a person in the pile still alive. But it was true. Incredibly, some of the corpses weren't corpses. They were human beings. We yelled for doctors, and they went to work on these survivors right away.*
>
> *I spent two hours in that boxcar, two hours that for me included every known emotion: rage, pity, shame, revulsion—every negative emotion, I should say. They came in waves, all but the rage. It stayed, fueling our work. We had no other emotional vocabulary for such a scene.*

Yancey's pastor friend said that it was then that God called him to the ministry. It was a profound urge to oppose the absolute evil that he found in the Dachau scene.

Yancey eventually asked a final question, "Tell me," he asked, "after such a cosmic kind of call to ministry—confronting the great evil of the century—how must it feel to fulfill that call by sitting in this office listening to middle-class yuppies like me ramble on about our personal problems?"

"I do see a connection," he answered. "Without being melodramatic, I sometimes wonder what might have happened if a skilled, sensitive person had befriended the young, impressionable Adolf Hitler as he wandered the streets of Vienna in his confused state. The world might have been spared all that bloodshed—spared Dachau. I never know who might be sitting in that chair you're occupying right now."[9]

Teachers—a potential Christlike human being is sitting in "that chair" right now. It may be in a Sunday School class, or at the kitchen table, or in a college algebra course. But be assured, they are there. The situation before us is simply this: Recognize the sobering challenge and then take a few hints from the One who desires that the occupant of that seat become all he or she was meant to be. "The better stuff a creature is made of," C.S. Lewis reminds us, "—the cleverer and stronger and freer it is—then the better it will be if it goes right, and also the worse it will be if it goes wrong."[10]

We are made of good—even the best—of stuff! But there is a responsibility that must ride tandem with that reality. In Haim Ginott's *Teacher and Child,* a school principal, the victim of the same kind of brutality described above, offered this to his teachers:

Dear teacher:

I am the survivor of a concentration camp. My eyes saw what no man should witness.

Gas chambers built by *learned* engineers.

Children poisoned by *educated* physicians.

Infants killed by *trained* nurses.

Women and babies shot and burned by *high school* and *college* graduates.

So, I am suspicious of education. My request is: Help your students become human. Your efforts must never produce learned monsters, skilled psychopaths, educated Eichmanns.

Reading, writing, arithmetic are important only if they serve to make our children more humane.[11]

THE MASTER PLAN OF TEACHING

To be as human as Jesus—whether your educational sphere of influence impacts students toward such an objective is wholly dependent on your allowing God to work through your gifts and graces. Be assured of this: It is the desire of the Almighty that we—and those we teach—go very right for Him. We need to be the skilled and sensitive teachers that Yancey's friend spoke of and God desires for us, for we never know the kind of influence the kingdom will feel because of our sensitivity to His plan.

Teachers are needed this hour—Jesus-like teachers. Apply today. And may God bless you in your efforts.

Beginning Steps...

1. *Of all the aspects of Jesus' teaching method discussed in this book, which comes easiest for you? Which is the most difficult? Are you ready to change? List specific steps you can take to adapt your style to Jesus'.*

2. *Look up Spirit in a concordance and make a list of all references to His teaching activity. Survey these passages. What promises does Scripture make? What responsibilities do we have in order to benefit from the Spirit's help?*

NOTES

Chapter One

[1]E. Stanley Jones, *A Song of Ascents* (New York/Nashville: Abingdon Press, 1968), 89.

[2]E. Stanley Jones, *The Christ of the Indian Road* (New York: Abingdon Press, 1925), 8–9.

[3]Frederick Mayer, *A History of Educational Thought* (Columbus, Ohio: Charles E. Merrill Books, Inc., 1966), 125, 129.

[4]*Encyclopedia Judaica,* 16 vols. (New York: Macmillan, 1972), s.v. "Jesus."

[5]Quoted in Charles H. Nichols, "An Analysis of the Teaching Methodology of Jesus Christ. . . ." (Ph.D. diss., University of Nebraska, 1983), 3.

[6]Jones, *Indian Road,* 19.

[7]George Gallup, Jr. and David Poling, *The Search for America's Faith* (Nashville: Abingdon Press, 1980), 48.

Chapter Two

[1]A.A. Milne, *Winnie the Pooh* (New York: Dell Publishing Co., 1954), 160.

[2]Dennis F. Kinlaw, "Holiness" in *Beacon Dictionary of Theology,* ed. Richard S. Taylor (Kansas City, Mo.: Beacon Hill Press, 1983), 36–37.

[3]Peter Berger, *A Rumor of Angels* (Garden City, N.J.: Anchor Books, 1970), 18–19.

⁴John Wesley, *Wesley's 52 Standard Sermons* (Salem, Ohio: Schmul Publishing Co., Inc., 1982), 237.

Chapter Three

¹I am indebted to Dennis Kinlaw for this thought represented in his book *Preaching in the Spirit* (Grand Rapids: Francis Asbury Press, 1985), 38.

²Eberhard Arnold, ed., *The Early Christians* (Grand Rapids: Baker Book House, 1979), 109–10.

³Quoted in E. Stanley Jones, *Christ and Human Suffering* (New York/Nashville: Abingdon/Cokesbury Press, 1933), 135.

⁴Clarence Jordan, *The Cotton Patch Version of Luke and Acts* (Chicago: Follett Publishing Company/Association Press, 1963), 46–47.

⁵George Seldes, comp. *The Great Thoughts* (New York: Ballantine Books, 1985), 285.

⁶Dr. Darrell Whiteman (professor at Asbury Theological Seminary), interview with author, April 1985.

⁷Darrell Whiteman, "Christian Witness and Culture" *The Asbury Herald,* 96:3 (Winter 1985), 3–6.

⁸Whiteman, interview

⁹John Jefferson Davis, *Foundations for Evangelical Theology* (Grand Rapids: Baker Book House, 1984), 50.

¹⁰Thomas Good and Jere Brophy, *Looking in Classrooms* (New York: Harper and Row, 1978), 119.

¹¹Based on Lawrence Richards, *A Theology of Christian Education* (Grand Rapids: Zondervan, 1975), 84–85.

¹²Quoted in Marvin Wilson's *Our Father Abraham: Jewish Roots of the Christian Faith* (Grand Rapids: William B. Eerdmans Publishing Co., 1989), 280.

Chapter Four

¹Richard Selzer, *Mortal Lessons: Notes on the Art of Surgery* (New York: Simon and Schuster, 1987), 45–46.

[2]Tom Sine, *The Mustard Seed Conspiracy* (Waco, Texas: Word Books, 1981), 11.

[3]Douglas Hyde, *Dedication and Leadership* (South Bend, Ind.: University of Notre Dame Press, 1966), 11.

[4]Dean Kelly, *Why Conservative Churches Are Growing* (New York: Harper and Row, 1972), 51.

[5]Margaret Magdalen, *Jesus, Man of Prayer* (Downers Grove, Ill.: InterVarsity Press, 1987), 75.

[6]Roger Ailes, *You Are the Message* (Homewood, Ill.: Dow Jones — Irwin, 1988), 5.

[7]Em Griffin, *Getting Together* (Downers Grove, Ill.: InterVarsity Press, 1982), 91.

[8]Colin Brown, ed., *The New International Dictionary of New Testament Theology, Vol. 3* (Grand Rapids: Zondervan Publishing House, 1971), 749.

[9]Stephen A. Grunlan and Marvin K. Mayers, *Cultural Anthropology: A Christian Perspective* (Grand Rapids: Academie Books/Zondervan Publishing House, 1979), 206.

[10]Win Arn, Donald McGavran, and Charles Arn, *Growth, A New Vision for the Sunday School* (Pasadena, Calif.: Church Growth Press, 1980), 76.

Chapter Five

[1]Robert Bretall, ed., *A Kierkegaard Anthology* (New York: Random House, 1946), 433.

[2]Ailes, *Message*, 47.

[3]Howard Hendricks, *Teaching to Change Lives* (Portland, Ore.: Multnomah Press, 1987), 81.

[4]Bretail, *Kierkegaard*, 19.

[5]Marvin Wilson, *Our Father Abraham: Jewish Roots of the Christian Faith*, (Grand Rapids: William B. Eerdmans Publishing Co., 1989), 288.

[6]Herman Horne, *The Teaching Techniques of Jesus* (Grand Rapids: Kregel Publications, 1976), 109–10.

[7]This case study is taken from Howard Hendricks (professor at Dallas Theological Seminary), interview with author, 22 December 1986.

[8]Hugh Evan Hopkins, *Charles Simeon of Cambridge* (London: Hodder and Stoughton, 1977), 59.

[9]Robert H. Waterman, Jr., *The Renewal Factor* (New York: Bantam Books, 1987), 26.

[10]Hyde, *Dedication and Leadership*, 56.

[11]Quoted in Elton Trueblood, *The Idea of a College* (New York: Harper and Row, 1959), 18.

[12]Ron Sider, *Rich Christians in an Age of Hunger* (Downers Grove, Ill.: InterVarsity Press, 1977), 66.

[13]Arnold, *The Early Christians*, 104.

[14]Paul Brand and Philip Yancey, *Fearfully and Wonderfully Made* (Minneapolis: Grason Company, 1981), 53–54.

[15]C.H. Spurgeon, *Lectures to my Students*, vol. I (Grand Rapids: Zondervan Publishing House, 1980), 78–79.

[16]Sally Reid, "Marva Collins: I Take the Kids No One Else Wants," *Instructor and Teacher*, January 1982, 18.

[17]Richard Foster, *Freedom of Simplicity* (New York: Harper and Row, 1981), 182.

[18]Charles Colson, *Presenting Belief in an Age of Unbelief* (Wheaton, Ill.: Victor Books, 1986), 26–27.

[19]*The Wall Street Journal*, 11 July 1980, p. 1, quoted in Jim Peterson, *Evangelism as a Lifestyle* (Colorado Springs, Colo.: NavPress, 1980), 84.

[20]Reprinted from the *Eye of the Needle* newsletter in *Leadership* (Winter 1987).

Chapter Six

[1]Holland McTyeire, *A History of Methodism* (Nashville: Barbee and Smith Agents, 1891), 204.

[2]D.W. Johnson, "Student-Student Interaction: The Neglected Variable in Education," *Educational Researcher* 10 (1981): 5.

[3]Gordon MacDonald, *Restoring Your Spiritual Passion* (Nashville: Oliver-Nelson, 1986), 198–99.

[4]Much of the following discussion is gleaned from Robert R. Blake and Jane S. Mouton, *The Managerial Grid III* (Houston: Gulf Publishing Company, 1985), 19–97.

[5]M. Scott Peck, *The Different Drum: Community Making and Peace* (New York: Simon and Schuster, 1987), 26.

[6]Kinlaw, *Preaching in the Spirit,* 39-40.

[7]Ibid.

[8]James Vance, *The College of the Apostles* (New York: Fleming H. Revell Company, 1896), 15-16.

[9]Foster, *Celebration of Discipline* (New York: Harper and Row, 1978), 156-57.

[10]Ibid., 155.

[11]Raphael Brown, *The Little Flowers of St. Francis* (Garden City, N.Y.: Image Books, 1958), 74–75.

[12]Louis Finkelstien, ed., *The Jews: Their History, Culture and Religion,* vol. 3 (New York: Harper and Brothers, 1949), 902–3.

[13]Jay Hall, "Decisions, Decisions, Decisions," *Psychology Today,* November 1971, 54.

[14]Hall, "Decisions," 86.

[15]Peck, *Different Drum,* 86ff.

[16]Linda Phillips-Jones, *Mentors & Proteges* (New York: Arbor House, 1982).

Chapter Seven

[1]Brookes More, trans., *Ovid's Metamorphoses,* vol. 2 (Francestown, N.H.: Marshall Jones Company, 1941), 474–77.

[2]George Bernard Shaw, *Pygmalion* (New York: Dodd, Mead, and Co., Inc., 1942). Quoted in Edward Kuhlman, *Master Teacher* (Old Tappan, N.J.: Fleming H. Revell Co., 1987), 117.

[3]Thomas Good and Jere E. Brophy, *Looking in Classrooms* (New York: Harper and Row, 1978), 67–70.

THE MASTER PLAN OF TEACHING

[4]Malcolm X, *The Autobiography of Malcolm X* (New York: Grove Press, 1964), 37.

[5]Anthony Campolo, "You Are Great in God's Eyes," (Pomona, Calif.: Focus on the Family, 1985).

[6]Kenneth Wydro, *Thinking on Your Feet* (Englewood Cliffs, N.J.: Prentice-Hall, 1981), 83. Wydro makes a different application of the same concept.

[7]"A Talk with the MacDonalds," *Christianity Today,* 10 July 1987, 38.

[8]A.B. Bruce, *The Training of the Twelve* (Grand Rapids: William B. Eerdmans Publishing Co., 1974), 14.

[9]Robert Coleman, *The Master Plan of Evangelism* (Old Tappan, N.J.: Fleming H. Revell, Co., 1963), 22–23.

[10]I am indebted to Allan Coppedge of Asbury Theological Seminary for this acrostic.

[11]David and Micki Colfax, *Homeschooling for Excellence* (New York: Warner Books, 1988), foreword.

[12]Gerald Mann, *Why Does Jesus Make Me Nervous?* (Waco, Texas: Word Books, 1980), 43.

[13]Elton Trueblood, *The Company of the Committed* (San Francisco: Harper and Row, 1980), 42-43.

[14]Foster, *Freedom of Simplicity,* 185.

[15]Lloyd C. Douglas, *The Robe* (Boston: Houghton, Mifflin, 1942), 302.

[16]Anthony Campolo, *Who Switched the Price Tags?* (Waco, Texas: Word Books, 1986), 195–97.

[17]Marva Collins and Civia Tamarkin, *Marva Collins' Way,* (Los Angeles: Jeremy P. Tarcher, Inc., 1982), 92.

[18]The following excerpts are from Collins and Tamarkin, 19-28.

[19]"Marva Collins: I Take the Kids No One Else Wants!" *Instructor and Teacher* (January 1982): 20.

[20]"Marva Collins—A Teacher Who Cares," *Good Housekeeping,* September 1978, 62.

[21]Collins and Tamarkin, 26.

²²Marlene LeFever, *Creative Teaching Methods* (Elgin, Ill.: David C. Cook Publishing Co., 1985), 116.

²³Thomas J. Peters and Robert H. Waterman, Jr., *In Search of Excellence* (New York: Warner Books, 1982), 84.

²⁴Cited in Jim Wilhoit, *Christian Education and the Search for Meaning* (Grand Rapids: Baker Book House, 1986), 132.

²⁵J. David Stone, *Spiritual Growth in Youth Ministry* (Loveland, Colo.: Group Books, 1985), 7–8.

Chapter Eight

¹Douglas, *Robe,* 379.

²Charles Colson, *The Role of the Church in Society* (Wheaton, Ill.: Victor Books, 1986), 18–19.

³Portions of this material gleaned from Ron Hembree, *Fruits of the Spirit* (Grand Rapids: Baker Book House, 1969), 79–80.

⁴Charles Swindoll, *Improving Your Serve* (Waco, Texas: Word Books, 1981), 34.

Chapter Nine

¹Quoted by John R.W. Stott, *Between Two Worlds* (Grand Rapids: William B. Eerdmans Publishing Co., 1982), 104.

²Friedrich Waismann, ed., *The Importance of Words* (Englewood Cliffs, N.J.: Prentice-Hall, Inc., 1962), 2.

³William Barclay, *The Gospel of Matthew,* vol. 1 of *The Daily Bible Study Series* (Philadelphia: The Westminster Press, 1975), 96.

⁴Arnold, *Early Christians,* 95.

⁵Anthony Parker, "For the Record," *Sojourners* (June 1989): 13.

⁶Roger Von Oech, *A Whack on the Side of the Head* (New York, Warner Books, 1983), 6.

⁷Fred B. Craddock, *As One without Authority* (Nashville: Abingdon Press, 1979), 60.

⁸Study by J. Bransford, cited in Jim Wilhoit, *Christian Education and the Search for Meaning,* (Grand Rapids: Baker Book House, 1987), 121–22.

[9]Quoted in Kenneth Gangel, *The Church Education Handbook* (Wheaton, Ill.: Victor Books, 1985), 28.

[10]William Bartlett, *Familiar Quotations* (Garden City, N.Y.: Garden City Publishing Co., Inc., 1944), 591.

[11]Ralph Lewis, *Inductive Preaching* (Westchester, Ill.: Crossway Books, 1983), 70.

[12]Ibid.

[13]Ibid., 71.

[14]"A Conversation with Benjamin Bloom," *Educational Leadership* (November 1979): 157.

[15]Von Oech, *Whack*, 97–98.

[16]Elton Trueblood, *The Humor of Christ* (San Francisco: Harper and Row, 1964), 10, 15.

[17]Ibid., 16.

[18]Elton Trueblood, *The Idea of a College* (New York: Harper and Row, 1959), 39.

Chapter Ten

[1]Betty Lee Skinner, *Daws* (Grand Rapids: Zondervan Publishing House, 1974), 82–83.

[2]Ibid., 77.

[3]John James Vincent, *Disciple and Lord: The Historical and Theological Significance of Discipleship in the Synoptic Gospels* (Sheffield, England: Academy Press, 1976), 114.

[4]C.S. Lewis, *Mere Christianity* (New York: MacMillan, 1952), 51.

[5]John M. Drescher, "A Parable of Fishless Fisherman," *Discipleship Journal*, Vol. 3:6 (November 1983): 42.

[6]Benjamin Bloom, "The Master Teachers," *Phi Delta Kappan* 63 (June, 1982): 664–68, 715.

[7]John Wesley, *Wesley's Works*, vol. 6 (Peabody, Mass.: Hendrickson Publishers, Inc., 1984), 199.

[8]Foster, *Celebration*, 1.

[9]George G. Hunter, *To Spread the Power* (Nashville: Abingdon Press, 1987), 113–114.